THE·FLIGHT·
OF·FEATHERED·SERPENT·

TEXT
AND ILLUSTRATIONS BY PETER BALIN

Also by PETER BALIN

The Xultun Tarot Deck.

The Way of the Sorcerer.

Acknowledgements

Editor, Richard Delap

Typesetting, Chiche Typesetting

Line Reproductions, Duographics Inc.

Printed by
Delta Lithograph Co.

FIRST EDITION   BY   WISDOM GARDEN BOOKS
SECOND EDITION BY   ARCANA PUBLISHING CO.
                    Box 2, Wilmot, Wisconsin 53192

LIBRARY OF CONGRESS CATALOG NO. 78-64357   10 9 8 7 6 5 4 3

ISBN 0-910261-01-6

INTRODUCTION

We may visit a friend as often as we wish, we need not know the address, indeed we don't even have to know the name of the town where the friend lives, all we need know is how to get there.

The Maya Indians are considered to have been the only civilization in the Americas that was fully literate. A great many glyphs of their writing system are clearly understandable to us, but we do not have the faintest glimmering of what words or spoken sense they conveyed. A great many of the place names can be recognized such as the one for Palenque, however it does not tell us what the Ancients called the city. Palenque is a Spanish word and means a Pallisade.

The whole reason that Maya science developed the great accuracy of their calendar, their mathematics, and astronomical knowledge was to record the progress of their history, the progress of their world for they believed as we do that history repeats itself (those who do not learn from history are doomed to repeat it). From the knowledge that history repeats itself comes the idea that one may be able to divine the future and so learn and prevent the making of the same mistakes over and over again. The arts of divination and prognostication were raised to unprecedented heights by the Maya. Unfortunately with the advent of the Europeans all of this knowledge has been lost, for the Europeans immured in their own superstitions believed it all to be the work of the devil, and so mounted a viscious and very successful campaign to eradicate the Indian sciences.

It seems that Mr. Balin has attempted to reconstruct the books of divination that guided the ancient priests in their tasks of survival. It is fairly obvious that we can never understand the sensitivities and feelings of these ancient peoples as they stood before the symbols of their religion. We are able to know the meaning of the glyphs simply because they speak to us on a level that is human, a level that is shared by all living intelligent beings.

The tarot speaks to us from this same level, the level of our fears and loves, our needs and desires, none of which would be foreign to the ancients. There is no doubt that an ancient Maya priest presented with a modern tarot deck would soon be able to work out its purpose and proceed to use it in precisely the same manner as we use it. It is unimportant where it originated, its style, or who made it, as none of this has anything to do with its function.

When an Indian from Central America, an Australian aborigine, or a New Zealand Maori enters into a state of trance, they are doing the same thing, they are going to the same place within the human psyche as did the oracles of Delos and Delphi.

By extension then the movement from divination (externalization) to self examination (internalization) is a logical progression. A knowledge of history leads one to a desire to control it on the one hand, so as to be free of it on the other. This desire to be free of the eternal repetition of events brings about the search for realization.

What Mr. Balin writes, using the Maya as a vehicle needs no verification, for each of us is able to verify the facts for ourselves. One can do no better than to quote from the Journey of the Fool,

> You are the book, search the self.
> Then shall secrets stand revealed.

The Publishers

CONTENTS

DEDICATION

The writer wishes to express his appreciation
to
JEAN LOUCKS   and to   DAVID BIEDEKAPP
for their confidence, friendship and love.

****

There are others, without whom the cards
would not have made their appearance
in the world

Frank Gaither

Netty Hess

Sam Hess

Tod Jonson

Lucenith Klomhaus

Jean Pape

Nathan Steinberg

Linda Seymour

Thank you one and all,
and thank you Marty Mitchnic,
a sorcerer whose little finger
points out the light.

TO YOU ALL ARE OFFERED THREE CUPS

In gratitude,

Peter Balin

THE·FLIGHT· OF·FEATHERED·SERPENT·

We are disenchanted with the world we have created. For a long time we thought that accumulating wealth would give us the security we so desire. We thought that technological power would enable us to manipulate the environment until our every wish was satisfied, and to ensure our safety, we built the ultimate weapon. For our pains we have found as much anxiety as contentment, and a great deal more chaos than order.

As mortal creatures we must die, and neither technology nor government can change this sufficiently to satisfy our needs. What is the use in the end of theories or promises? Of what avail are our beliefs when we want certainty? How can we maintain integrity when our contrived sources of energy tear us to pieces?

Dissatisfaction in life, the fear of death, the search for knowledge that we believe will set us free—all these are dealt with in the tarot. The tarot is a unique and accessible instrument by which we gain awareness of the ever-changing view we have upon the accident of our being. There is no direct, easy, or instant road to realization. The truth, if one is to accept it, is that there is no path, save that which each one of us alone may create.

Realization and all that it implies is what the tarot is about. If we are to understand life and death, we must understand time. If we are to understand the self, we must surrender all ownership of likes and dislikes. Above all we must want with the whole heart and mind to know what is, and this entails surrendering all ideas we have about it, all images, all views, for these are trauma and give direct rise to all suffering.

Most of us want to be free, yet we feel bound and tied to various situations. Our desire for freedom is a reaction to our bondage and that is also a truth. We want freedom from poverty, from suffering, from disease and death, and our want for freedom is always a reaction: we want FREEDOM FROM SOMETHING. If we examine this concept carefully, we observe that this sort of freedom is not freedom at all. Any reaction is forever tied to its cause and all bonds are a lack of freedom. To be free one must act. There cannot be any reaction. What is the difference between the two? Can we understand all this? Is it just semantics?

Thousands of books outline all of our problems, delineate them and supply us with answers. Why do they make so little difference in our lives? It is not this writer's intention to answer any of these questions here in the foreword, or indeed anywhere else, for that is not the book's function. The aim is to deal with life as it is lived by each one of us in our incredible diversity and to present the material in such a way that at the end of the process YOU UNDERSTAND YOU.

Recently there has been a tremendous upsurge of interest in the tarot, and that is a good thing (at least it certainy is for people like myself, who have designed tarot decks and who write books about the tarot). The reason may well be that tarot fulfills a need, and as more people discover this need within themselves, their response is to find a way to satisfy the need.

Mankind's reaction to pain is a sort of internalized fight or flight response, so in reaction to a desire to comprehend oneself, which is a response to flight from discomfort on one hand and an image of freedom from the discomfort on the other, we take up the tarot. When used properly, the tarot is an investigatory tool, a detective's magnifying glass, a psychologist's Rorschach test. With the tarot it may be possible to see that the concept of comfort resides only in the head and not at all in the body. (Observe children and cats: they do not *seek* comfort, yet they always are finding it.)

The tarot deals with the necessity of seeing oneself as a whole, not separate from the world around us, not fragmented. We usually think of ourselves as separate from others—I AM ME, or to paraphrase the famous dictum, "I think I am, therefore the I is." Because we think like this, it is so. In this way we bring about a separatist world, a world in which each one of us thinks of ourselves as isolated identities, connected to each other only by needs: food, clothing, shelter, sex.

It is the function of the tarot to change this situation. It must be understood, however, that the tarot can *do* nothing. It is just a bunch of pretty pictures, arranged in a particular order. Everything is done by the one who uses the tarot. This is possible because the user has first built up a repertoire of images, the changing nature of which is comprehended by the user, much as one would do when looking through a collection of photographs depicting several generations of a family. Recognition would occur but the verbalizations would be of little understanding to anyone listening. There would be many exclamations because pictures convey their meanings on different levels to different parts of the brain, yet no amount of description can convey all the innuendo, all the implication of a picture. One picture speaks a thousand words.

Societal change cannot be dictated into being. Essential change is an individual and personal matter. As I come to be aware of the complexity of myself and my actions, this awareness tells me that others are just as complex. My awareness has now become part of the society and the society as a whole is more aware. Societies are not separate from the individuals that make them up.

The use of the tarot calls for a 'detached watching,' which in the East is called meditation. In the Western world it is called contemplation. This does not imply a process of absorbed interest, a form of hypnosis wherein the mind slowly shuts down and focuses in on an ever-diminishing point thought of as the center of the being. This meditation is quite the reverse process. It is difficult to describe, but perhaps it could be called a watchful open enquiry, wherein the mind first must allow total freedom to discover. There is a complete openness that allows the truth, whatever that may be, to shine forth.

There can be no understanding of the self if there is any acceptance or rejection in the action. One will want to continually judge what occurs. Observe! One will be continually for or against whatever is revealed. This is the movement of our lives. Observe! Eventually, as awareness comes, there will be a quiet, dispassionate something that is doing the watching, a sense of one's awareness as a being. One is always surprised by awareness, for everything is always new. The discovery of one's intelligence seems to be what occurs. It is an intelligence that has no interest in how long the process takes, for no matter what one may think, all "seeing" takes place in the instant.

It is a well-known fact that we use less than one-eighth of our mental potential. It is also known that intelligence cannot be learned in a classroom; neither can it be enlarged by reading or study. Intelligence is developed in spontaneous, accidental insight. The word "intelligence" is made of two Latin words: *inter*, which means between, and *legere*, meaning line. Therefore, the word intelligence means *to see between the lines*—that is, to be able to see what is actually happening around oneself rather than be caught up in one's hopes, wishes and desires; to be able to see what is actually happening in any given situation without becoming entangled in its symbolic representation.

Far too many of us spend our lives in confusion, or in a haze of indifference, unable to understand what goes on around us, unaware of how the world operates. This strange turn of

events seems to have little to do with education or position in the society, and it can bode nothing but ill for a society that is governed by the mass will.

The tarot is a way to develop the ability to see "what is," which often includes what we would like it to be. All of it is part of "what is actually happening," and so our lives begin to balance, begin to manifest harmony and wisdom. The strange thing about certain human conditions such as intelligence, harmony, wisdom, joy or love, is that whenever they manifest, they are complete, they are not fragmented. One is wise, not getting wiser and wiser. One is joyful, not becoming more and more joyful. One gives love, not a little love. It seems that a certain aspect of the human condition is not amenable to degrees. It is or it isn't, and that is that, regardless of who says it.

The tarot is an ancient set of symbols arranged in two decks of cards, one containing 22 cards and the other 56 cards. The first deck of 22 cards is called the HIGHER ARCANA (the word arcana means mystery) and is, so to speak, a concentration of the 56 cards, called

the LOWER ARCANA. This second deck again divides into the Court cards, being 16 cards with persons represented on them: Lords, Ladies, Servants, and Warriors. The remaining 40 cards divide into four suits. The first, called STAFFS, tells of one's spiritual aspirations, hopes, and desires. The second is called SWORDS, and they tell of the mental aspirations and capabilities. The third suit is called CUPS, and it deals with the emotions and their complications. The last suit is called JADES, and it encompasses the physical existence of a person.

In a layout, or SPREAD, it can easily be seen that the reader is presented with an almost endless number of arrangements of cards that combine to produce an unparalleled variety of accidental relationships. It is in the observation of these relationships that the true work of the tarot is done. When proficiency at recognizing symbolic values in accidental relationships is developed, we have created an exact model of the universe from our unique position in it. This model is then available for observation and experimentation to whatever degree, or to the limits of whatever our capacity is.

With the tarot, our limitations are always where we start, as it is where we start in the world. We stand a better chance at a joyful, wise and loving life if we understand from where we are coming and if we are openly aware of the limitations we harbor. In this manner, then, the tarot functions to give us proficiency in reading relationships, not just personal relationships, but relationships within groups and things. The word *real* means the world of things, so we must look carefully at "relationship" and what it means. Relationship is the meeting of different things, often based upon a need of some sort or another. If I borrow money from you, we have a relationship. The citizen is in relationship with the nation, the patient with the doctor, the wife with the husband. Where we want something from each other or fulfil a need for each other we are in relationship. All of us spend our entire lives in relationship, or better yet (no worse), searching for the ideal relationship.

The tarot shows us a view of the fascinating,

intriguing, ever-changing, ever-new, wonderfully unique person that each of us is. And the inevitable result of this is love, for love begins with the self. If one finds oneself an absolute delight, how can one fail to find others in their wonderful uniqueness equally delightful. Love is total freedom. In love there can be no relationship. For love is a total and absolute communion with the real, regardless of how it manifests. In love there is no desire to change anything, but rather allowing change to take place in its own way. In love there is no relationship. There is freedom, harmony, and wisdom, none of which can be learned and like intelligence comes about in the instant when we have worked the hardest and are least prepared.

Proficiency in "reading" is a gradual process, one in which speed and insight are always controlled by the reader. The insights gained are only the "view" of the reader, and the reader is perpetually changing. The only limitation is the imagination of the reader of the cards, and the only exercise is to extend this imagination. Imagination is the edge of the mind, the boundary between brain and mind in

its harmonious functioning, which is called intelligence. The brain may be put under a microscope and examined, but not the mind. The tarot exercises the mind in reading between the lines; it uses play to develop an unshackled perception of what is. What is understood in the use of the tarot is outside the field of learning, for it enables the reader to step beyond the limitations of mind and stand at the source of the world of form.

The tarot has nothing to do with sorcery or witchcraft as it is generally understood. It has nothing to do with the casting of evil spells. A SORCERER, according to the dictionary, is one who opposes fate; one who stands at the source. We now can see that the creative person is really the sorcerer. People who react need a cause, a reason to act, and when that is lacking they remain passive. Life passes them by simply because they are not part of life. They remain separate, neatly bundled up in their little cocoon of fate. A sorcerer is one who initiates action, one who is a doer, as opposed to the person who only reacts.

Life to the creative individual is a mixture of fate and design, it is only with an alertness to the moment that we may overcome the past and action take place. It is only in the now that we are free of fate and our actions are loving. Love is not a word, it is a way of action and action is now. Now is, it is not a process of becoming, for becoming is fear and in love there can be no fear.

The

Many cultures have held the human skull in high esteem as a symbol of potent ability.

And what is a symbol? The word has its origin in the Greek language (*symbolon*), and came to represent a token of identity that could be verified by comparison with its other half. The modern meaning of SYMBOL is as a visible sign of something invisible: an act, sound, or object having a cultural significance and the capacity to excite or objectify a response through unconscious association. As with words that are continually used and the meaning taken for granted, however, an error of significance creeps in. Often the word is used the same as the word CYPHER, which simply means a sign that stands for a thing or complex idea, an example of which would be this cypher O, which stands for the concept of zero, or that nothing can be given a value which represents nothing. Drawn below is a symbol that everyone will recognize. Look at it carefully and see all of the ideas and associations that spring to mind.

Symbolism of The Skull

An Aztec skull with the glyphs burning water *issuing from the mouth and on the crown the glyph* Smoking Mirror.

The above symbol has the ability to excite ideas because over a long period Western society has invested it with particular responses, from the idea of industry to all sorts of social implications. Yet there is probably only a handful of people who have ever seen such an object—and certainly very few people would know what it is made of. The object, of course, is a beehive, yet it ceased to be used in this form more than a hundred years ago. It was made of straw woven into a thick rope that was then twined into this upside-down cup shape and coated with mud. The honeycomb was hung from the center and a small arched opening was made on one side at the bottom. The fact that one may never have actually seen this object and does not know of what it is made does not in any way diminish its potency as a symbol. (The drawing, by the way, is taken from one of those plastic measured-portion containers of honey served up in chain restaurants.)

The skull and crossbones seen on poison bottles in some parts of the world, and also seen on electric power poles, is an example of the skull being used as a cypher, and meaning death. As a symbol it is much more profound, less significant of death than of another realm, a world where only the bare bones, stripped of the flesh that makes an individual, may enter. This is a world of equality, where worldly goods have no account—witness Hamlet's speech to the skull in the graveyard. It has the association of bare essentials, of an empty house, of the absolute truth. A speaking skull presents one with a bizarre image of contradiction and causes a fascination that is a combination of curiosity and terror. It carries the idea of separation, lack of ease, and a certain harmony of proportion and stark beauty, that over many civilizations has caused it to be used as drinking cups and candle holders, such use being obviously symbolic, the filling and emptying of the life force, the light from darkness concept with its hint at initiation ceremonies, etc.

Within the Egyptian symbolic system it was the crown of the skull that seemed to convey to them an idea that only in recent time is finding renewed acceptance. In drawings from this civilization, the crown is invariably separated from the rest of the head by a band, a diadem, or fillet. This separation is sometimes the joint between the stones upon which the image is carved. When we examine this part of the skull that is detached, we find that it contains the two hemispheres of the brain. These hemispheres of the cerebrum are made up of the outer layer called the cortex or mantle, the gray matter of the brain, and under that is the white mass separated by a layer of nerve fibers. It is from the cortex and the two lobes of the brain that all orders for the actions of the body proceed.

Those who wish to investigate this fascinating subject further will find helpful books listed in the bibliography, but for now I will attempt to outline in general how the two lobes of the brain function, for it is this understanding that will make clear to us the significance the skull has for the ancient peoples of both Europe and the Americas. It may be a meaning that also has deep significance for us today.

The left and right hemispheres of the brain are separated from each other by a fibrous cartilage shaped like the blade of a sickle, which ossifies (that is, turns brittle and bone-like) with age. This cartilage not only acts as a separator in fact, but also symbolically, for it divides that part of the cerebrum which houses reason, intellectualizing functions and speech, from those of idea and unifying functions.
Put more simply, the left or dominant hemisphere looks only at the parts of things, takes them apart, and speaks about them. The right hemisphere sees the parts of things as having a mening only within a context, and literally sings about them. With most people, including most left-handed people, the dominant side of the brain is the left hemisphere, although with some left-handed people the placement is reversed. Sometimes the Dominant hemisphere (left) is called the masculine and the Passive hemisphere (right) is called the femiminine. The industrial revolution resulted from the hard-line left-brain manner of thought, and our society has continued to develop along this line.

Perhaps left-brain activity is best seen as a railway line, coming from the past and proceeding into the bright and golden future that always waits before us. This railway line has thousands of boxcars, all separate from each other and labeled plainly: biology, astronomy, psychology, etc. All left-brain activity insists upon being kept separate from other activity because it is from this separation that it derives its strength and power. On the other hand, right-brain activity (and societies) may best be described as a bright light that shines forth in all directions from a center. Since it is concerned with synthesis, it is long-enduring, open, all-inclusive. It expresses itself in architecture, sculpture, music, poetry and song. Its science is always of the inclusive variety, such as astrology, numerology, the study of the construction and meaning of the alphabet, and, of course, the tarot.

Bearing these descriptions in mind, and the idea that all societies prior to 1000 B.C. were in all probability right-brain societies, the story in the Bible about the war in heaven achieves added significance—not the triumph of good over bad, but the triumph of the left brain and the banishment of the right brain. The one cast out of heaven was LUCIFER, whose name means the light bringer.

In this manner of thought, the Biblical description of the fall from grace also seems revelatory. Adam was alone in the garden, whole, complete, undivided, possessed of a unique and direct intelligence. Then Eve was created, separated from Adam's rib (one may describe the fibrous division between the brain as having a sickle or rib shape), and into his life enters contradiction and with it the possibility of knowledge. First we have Adam sharing the divine nature, then his fall into the natural world of opposition, good and evil, birth and death. Adam no longer understands by merging with the creative mystery; he only has understanding through the comparison of opposites.

The beautiful skull drawn at the head of this chapter is taken from the depiction of a large ball on a temple wall at Chichen Itza. Such balls were used in ball games played throughout the ancient Americas, and ball courts have been found in such places as Arizona and Ohio. The skull has a Speech Scroll issuing from the mouth, and the cross on it means darkness, more precisely the darkness of the planet Venus, meaning that time of eight days when it is not visible, between its setting as an evening star and its rising as a morning star. The sign behind the ear is the symbol of SMOKING MIRROR, the opposite, the god who was the perpetual rival of FEATHERED SERPENT, who is the personification of the

planet Venus.

The other drawing is a later version done by the Aztec civilization. Issuing from the mouth is a scroll with the glyphs for fire and water written on it. Again on the back of the head is the symbol of Smoking Mirror. By this time, some five hundred years after the first skull, the Aztecs worshipped Smoking Mirror as their principal deity, yet they never entirely deserted Feathered Serpent, for he always had his temple on the great pyramid at Tenochtitlan, next to the blood-stained temple of Smoking Mirror.

The skull, then, is a potent symbol for the contradiction in which people throughout the ages have passed their lives. It is the exact representation of the world of nature where, at least on this planet, all energy expresses itself in dualism. There is no electricity without the two poles, no continuation of the species without the two sexes, and possibly no human culture without the basic concept upon which all other concepts rely, darkness and light for it

is only when we perceive the negative pole that the positive pole is created. We may not know exactly what love is, but we certainly recognize what it is *not*.

Left-brain cultures rise and fall with great rapidity and tremendous destruction. Observe how within the last ten years a very decided decline has set in. It seems that almost everything we do as a society hastens the probable end.

The tarot is one of the few right-brain products that seems to bridge the abyss that separates the two hemispheres. The applied correct use of the tarot definitely makes right-brain activity plausible to the left brain, and just may bring about in individuals a harmonious, once more divine understanding of the world around us. It may quiet the soul and silence once and for all that nagging human question . . . why?

The Legend of Feathered

THE GREAT TEACHER AND REDEEMER OF THE PEOPLES

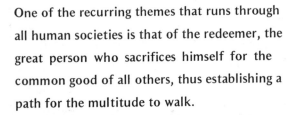

The myth appears to speak of the blossoming of an individual soul, which can attain to a superior, liberating consciousness through painful human experience in which sin—the dark side of corporeal life—is as necessary as the bright side.

Laurette Sejourne, *Burning Water*

One of the recurring themes that runs through all human societies is that of the redeemer, the great person who sacrifices himself for the common good of all others, thus establishing a path for the multitude to walk.

Feathered Serpent taught that human greatness grows out of awareness, that awareness is the source of all order, and that order flows from awareness when there is virtue. He taught that self-understanding flowered in the human mind and its fruits were love and joy. He taught that love was the source of all technique. He raised craft, that is, operating in the natural world, to the level of communion with the divine.

Almost a thousand years before the birth of Christ he walked the Americas, teaching as he went. To the Inca people of South America he was known as VIRACOCHA. To the Mayas of Yucatan, he was KUKULCAN, and to the Mayas in Guatamala he was GUKUMATZ. Feathered Serpent is more familiar to us today by the name the Aztec people called him, QUETZALCOATL, which is the Nahua language, the tongue adopted by the Aztecs when they gave up their own language.

All of these names have the same meaning: Feathered Serpent. It is a title bestowed upon this great teacher in much the same way as the title Christ (the anointed one) was given to Joshua Bar Joseph, the Jewish carpenter, or Buddha (enlightened one) was given to the young Hindu Prince Siddhartha Gautama.

The name Quetzalcoatl is a three-part name. The word *quetzal* means precious green, bird, or feather; *co* is the generic name for serpent; and the word *atl* means water. It fits together like this: the feathers of the bird, the creature that inhabits the highest element, are joined to the body of the water snake, a creature of the lowest element. The name is a graphic description of realization, the highest and the lowest expressed harmoniouslywithin the one body.

It is quite a difficult task to separate the historical Feathered Serpent from the myth that surrounds him through his different appearances upon the earth. Perhaps it is necessary to state that the Maya people believed in the theory of rebirth, but whether it was similar to the Hindu concept of reincarnation is hard to say. The Mayas seemed to believe that not every soul was reborn but only those who had a special work to do. Particular emphasis was put upon *now*, for it was understood that how

Serpent
OF THE AMERICAS

one acted in the moment to the challenge of life was what formed the new life to which one would be born. Since Feathered Serpent had taken on the work of redeeming humanity, he would have to return again and again until the work was accomplished.

Images of Feathered Serpent form the principal decoration at the ancient city of Teotihuacan. Yet predating Teotihuacan his image appears carved in stone and is all that remains of the Olmec civilization, which seemed to flower around Veracruz, on the gulf of Mexico. Very little is known about these people, except that they probably were the precursors of civilization in the Americas, and particularly of Maya civilization.

The great teacher taught that human sacrifice was wrong. He taught of an ordered society in which the least of its members would be able to find an expression for themselves, a framework of order derived from knowledge of the crafts. Feathered Serpent is thought of as the great culture hero, for he was an architect, a potter, an astronomer and an astrologist. He is credited with the invention of writing and the calendar. The more one learns of this teacher the more difficult it becomes not to compare him with Saint Francis, the great humanist of Christianity and the closest to approach the status of a realized teacher of Western civilization.

Historically, the succession of persons known as Feathered Serpent begins about one hundred B.C., when he established his capital at Chichen Itza (mouth of the well of the Itza). The city flourished for three or four hundred years, then for reasons unknown was abandoned and fell into ruins. The second Feathered Serpent was born in about the 9th century at Tula, the growing center of the Toltec people. (With the word *Toltec* we encounter one of the confusing names given to ancient Mexican cultures. Toltec simply means "the builders," and they probably were related to the Maya culture, for it is recorded that they spoke Maya with an accent, probably a dialect.)

Ce-Acatl Topiltzin, for that was his name, was

A PORTRAIT OF CE-ACATL TOPILTZIN
This drawing is taken from the temple of Quetzal-coatl at Chichen Itza, where there are several portraits of Feathered Serpent sculptured in stone, including one in advanced old age. Note the turtle shell used as clothing; it alludes to Itzamna (Morning Dew) the first Feathered Serpent, who came from the sea to establish Chichen in ancient times.

born into a culture on the rise, and he became the instrument of great strife within the city of Tula. Great military cults were beginning to establish themselves and they worshipped his great rival, Smoking Mirror. Ce-Acatl means one reed and is his calendar name, for it is the year in which he was born and the year in which at his death he said he would return. One Reed was famous for his charity and his chastity, for his ability to teach, and above all for the great beauty of his doctrine.

Matters eventually came to a head between the priests grown powerful through military cults devoted to Smoking Mirror and craftsman cults devoted to Feathered Serpent. Feathered Serpent at last left Tula—although it is not clear whether he was driven away or left voluntarily—taking with him large numbers of craftsmen. They began to wander.

Feathered Serpent and his followers then settled at the city of Chichen, then in ruins and abandoned for four hundred years. They rebuilt the old buildings and made new ones, including a new temple for Feathered Serpent. It was identical in style to the temple built by Morning Dew, over which it was constructed, covering it completely and preserving it against the ravages of time. We know he did this because he left several likenesses of himself on the temple, an important one being carved on the side of the principal door, where he is depicted as holding up the lintel, in effect saying, "I caused this to be done." With this action of preserving the temple of Morning Dew within his own temple, he established his claim as the incarnation of Feathered Serpent.

The city grew and flourished and he succeeded in welding the Mayas into a federation of states, with its capital at Mayapan (standard of the Maya), a city newly built in the style of Chichen. But the military cultism that was spreading like wildfire throughout the whole of the Americas threatened to overwhelm the city of Chichen, and Feathered Serpent, now an old man, decided to leave.

He left the city with a few followers, some say in disgrace after having been made drunk by the followers of Smoking Mirror, who persuaded him to have sexual intercourse with his own sister. However he left the city, legend says that he and his followers built a huge fire in which he immolated himself. Legend also says that a flock of birds lifted his soul to heaven after first going through the underworld, where he remained for eight days. Finally he rose triumphant as the morning star, the planet Venus. Before he left he prophesied his return in the year one reed, vowing he would then destroy the work of Smoking Mirror.

After his death the cities began to disintegrate, and by the time the Spaniards arrived nothing was left, for the Mayas had split into small tribes, fighting and squabbling among themselves. They had enough strength, however, to defeat the Spaniards on several occasions, and the conquest of the Mayas took eighty years.

One of the interesting coincidences of history is that when Cortez arrived and defeated the Aztec people, it was the year of Ce-Acatl, the exact year in which the prophecy said Feathered Serpent would return. Many believe that Cortez was an incarnation of Feathered Serpent, and that he came and destroyed everything that was the work of Smoking Mirror.

In time the fourth Feathered Serpent would make himself known and repair the damage done by the third Feathered Serpent. This would be the time of the end of the fifth sun.

We can see that the legend deals with a cyclical event, the ever-recurring incarnation of the redeemer, who moves people slowly but surely toward the position of oneness with the gods. The Mayas taught that as man is mortal, so are the gods, but as the life of the gods is inconceivable to mortal man, so also the mortality of the gods is inconceivable. The American Indian peoples felt that one must live in harmony with the gods and the attributes through which they express themselves: the climate, the seasons, the rain or lack of it. They felt that within this cycle a great balance is created, that to store up goods for the morrow is a denial that the godhead is cognizant of what is occurring.

During times of starvation, populations die and fall back to a level which can be supported by the food available. The old die, the sick die, the very young die. As more food becomes available, so the population grows, things become better. This great movement of harmony is considered far more important than individual survival.

The recurring appearance of the redeemer, who slowly and inexorably is creating a society wherein all things are in balance, is the magnificent expression of this legend. It does not treat of an evolving situation but of a recurring one. It would seem that Feathered Serpent teaches the true worth of the doctrine of Smoking Mirror by allowing the people to experience life under the sway of the War God. He allows them to see what happens and permits them to suffer the consequences.

Since the doctrine treats fundamentally of freedom and of learning, all of which is expressed in awareness, so the redeemer interferes only in a negative way with the course

that human beings choose. The incarnation as Cortez falls within this context, for his appearance was an appointing of the way for a society that was based on the teachings of the War God.

There is a very beautiful story of the life of Ce-Acatl Topiltzin told by Jose Lopez Portillo, the president elect of Mexico, who writes with great sensitivity of the incarnation of Quetzalcoatl. His telling of the story of Feathered Serpent synthesizes not only the teachings of this most benevolent of Mexican teachers, but also the legends and teachings of all great religious leaders from Buddha to Christ. From the history of the conquest of Mexico, and especially the account of Montezuma II, we begin to realize how the Spanish Conquistadors were able to brutally enslave an entire nation, while the Indians who thought the invasion to be the promised second coming of their god king, Feathered Serpent, made no attempt to defend themselves until it was too late.

The Surviving Writings of The Maya

THE BOOKS OF CHILAM BALAM, THE POPOL VUH AND THE FOUR REMAINING

These people also made use of certain characters or letters, with which they wrote in their books their ancient affairs and sciences, and with these and drawings and with certain signs in these drawings, they understood their affairs and made others understand them and taught them. We found a great number of books in these characters, and, as they contained nothing in which there was not to be seen superstition and lies of the devil, we burned them all, which they regretted to an amazing degree and which caused them affliction.

Relación de las Cosas de Yucatán
Diego de Landa.

The foregoing passage is from Bishop Landa 's book, *Relacion de las Cosas de Yucatán*, which he wrote in prison after he was recalled to Spain for having overstepped his authority in burning the books of Mexico. Not every book was burned. Until recently it was thought that only three ancient codexes survived, but a fourth and quite remarkable one was discovered, under unknown circumstances, in about 1970. A few other books of the Mixtec and Aztec people also survived.

The Mayas had developed a civilization incredibly advanced in intellectual accomplishments, and scholars still bemoan the auto-da-fe perpetrated with such zeal by the Christian clergy. We have still not solved the riddle of the Maya glyphs, although some can be understood, principally those having to do with mathematics. Other glyphs, some having to do with personal names and place names, are understood, although their translation into sound is less sure. Some of it is thought to be analogous to rebus, or pun writing. An example in English is:

I   SAW   YOU

There is no general agreement about this, however, for some people believe that phonetic elements are part of the writing. It is possible that the glyphs are a mixture of many different elements, for there is a strange universality about the Mayan culture. Their intellectual reasoning made use of many complex elements and combined these elements into a system which was varied and open.

The difficulty facing scholars is that the successful translation of one glyph does not seem to help at all with the translation of other glyphs. Even the translated glyph in a different arrangement may not have a clear meaning.

The Mayas are often thought of as being obsessed with time; it is not this writer's opinion at all. Their relationship with the phenomena of time was more as an anchor for their history and learning, linked to a method of keeping track of the movements of heavenly bodies.

The Maya concept of time springs from totally different sources, one completely unlike our obsessive abstraction, the basis of which is at the root of the Industrial Revolution. It is we who are obsessed with the division of time as a means of power and control—witness the railroad, bus and airplane timetables, the vast proliferation of clocks, radios, alarms, working hours, and television schedules (and let's not forget the parking meters!). To demonstrate that the Mayas' concern with time was of a ritual importance in the recording of their history, we have extant two time calculations. The first records a period going back ninety million years and represents an extraordinary feat of observation and calculation.

Priests.

MAYA CODICES.

This other glyph goes back even further, four hundred million years!

What were such calculations used for? No one knows. They required a vast quantity of man hours to produce, possibly several lifetimes. There may have been even more ancient ones, painted on wooden markers that have not survived in the damp tropical climate. It is believed that the present cycle of time, the fifth creation, had its beginning in 3113 B.C., although the Grolier codex seems to support the date 3374 B.C. (There is much debate among students as to just when the calendar had its beginning.)

There are two books written soon after the conquest. They were written in Roman script by priests who had learned it from the missionaries. The books of Chilam Balam, that is, the books of the Jaguar priest, are from the Yucatan and are a collection of prophecies. Sometimes the principal book, the Chilam Balam of Chumayel, is called the book of the Prophet Balam.

The Prophet Balam lived during the last years of the fourteenth century. He foretold the coming of strangers from the East who would force a new religion onto the people. The prompt fulfillment of this prophecy with the coming of the Spaniards so enhanced his reputation that many other prophecies uttered long before his time were attributed to him.

The Chumayal has been translated into English and is indeed a book of prophecy. There is great difficulty in following it, however, for it uses no punctuation at all and the prophecies are complex. Here is the prophecy (translated) concerning the coming of the second Feathered Serpent:

KATUN 4 AHAU is the eleventh katun according to the count. The katun is established at Chichen Itza. The settlement of the Itza is there. The quetzal, the precious green bird shall come. Ah Kantenal shall come. Feathered Serpent shall come with them for a second time. It is the word of God he shall come to the Itza.

The Katun 4 Ahau is a time period and it occurred in about the tenth century.

Here is another prophecy concerning the end of the fifth sun, the present time period—somehow it has a familiar ring to it.

The Earth shall burn and there shall be a circle in the sky. Food shall be set up; He shall be set up in front in time to come. It shall burn on earth; the very feet shall burn in that katun, in the time which is to come. Fortunate are they who shall hear this prophecy declared, for then, all shall weep over this misfortune in the time to come.

Next is a prophecy that probably deals with the third coming of Feathered Serpent. It is the prophecy of the singer Chilam Balam of Cabalchen.

THE GROLIER CODEX: Four pages of a newly discovered book dealing with 1352 years of the cycles of the planet Venus. (Drawn after a photograph that appeared in the New York Times.)

There is the sign of the living incorporeal and true God on high. The raised wooden standard shall come. It shall be displayed to the world, that the world may be enlightened, lord. There has been a beginning of strife, there has been a beginning of rivalry, when the priestly man shall come to bring the sign of Feathered Serpent, in time to come, lord. The distance of a cry away, he comes. You see the precious bird surmounting the raised wooden standard. A new day shall dawn in the north, in the west. The one true God shall rise. Our Lord comes. Our elder brother comes, all you people receive your guest, the bearded man, the men of the East, the bearers of the sign of God,

lord.

The prophecies have a great beauty about them, and like most prophecies will only be understood in retrospect. They certainly give a feeling of deep respect and wisdom. There is nothing primitive about them.

The Popol Vuh, or the book of Council, is another book written in Roman script, but it comes from Guatamala. Written about the same time as the Chilam Balam, it is more a history of the Quiche Maya people, although it does contain the creation story and many other beautiful stories of a religious nature. Both this book and the Yucatan book survived because they were kept secret. The author or authors of the Popol Vuh are unknown.

The three ancient codexes were all discovered in Europe. The Dresden codex is in the Royal Library at Dresden. Madrid possesses a codex believed to have crossed the ocean with Cortez; it is known as the Codex Cortesianus and is probably a book of horoscopes, which the priests used in making divinations. The Paris or Perez codex was found in 1860 in the National Library in Paris. It is only a fragment and seems to be concerned with ceremonies and divination.

A fourth codex surfaced in 1971. It was displayed in New York at the Grolier Club and has since been known by the club's name. It is considered to be the most important of all the codexes and has been called "the world's first and only known perpetual calendar of Venus ever produced by any civilization." Another authority goes on to say, "This ancient Mayan document must rank among the supreme intellectual achievements of human history."

What a remarkable people the Mayas were!

Their achievements, it must be noted, were not *only* intellectual. They invented concrete, practiced tailoring (a very unusual thing for a

All moons, all years, all days, all winds,
Reach their completion and pass away.
So does all blood reach its place of quiet,
As it reaches its power and its throne.

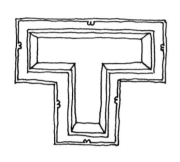

Measured is the time in which
We can praise
the splendour of the trinity.
Measured is the time in which
We can know the suns benevolence.
Measured is the time in which
The grid of the stars looks down upon us
And through it,
keeping watch over their safety
The gods traped within the stars
Measure their fate.

The Popol Vuh

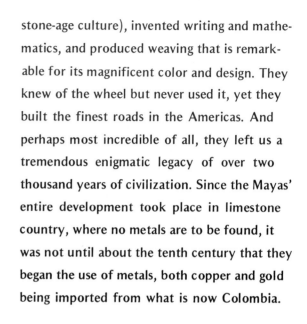

stone-age culture), invented writing and mathematics, and produced weaving that is remarkable for its magnificent color and design. They knew of the wheel but never used it, yet they built the finest roads in the Americas. And perhaps most incredible of all, they left us a tremendous enigmatic legacy of over two thousand years of civilization. Since the Mayas' entire development took place in limestone country, where no metals are to be found, it was not until about the tenth century that they began the use of metals, both copper and gold being imported from what is now Colombia.

The Maya culture is vital and alive, more and more claiming the attention of Western scholars. Who knows . . . the answers to the questions and problems of our modern world may lie among the silent cities of the Mayas. The West has always been good at selecting and adapting its civilization from other peoples. Our government is modeled after Rome, as is our military. Our religion is taken from the Jews, our psychology from the Greeks, our mathematics from the Arabs, and our science had its beginnings with the Italians, as did our art. What may we find useful among these refined and godly people's culture, that may serve us in good stead?

The Creation Myth

This myth is common among the original American peoples. It has been adapted to each locale, from the respected Hopis of Arizona to the Eskimo peoples, as well as most of the peoples of South America, but the myth varies only slightly, and it goes something like this:

The Gods came together in darkness, for nothing that is now was yet in existence. All was emptiness, all was darkness, all was potential. To keep themselves amused, the Gods decided to create the world and set to work in great seriousness. They argued and pondered and discussed, and then they created the first sun, the first world. It was pure spirit, fire and energy and heat. It had a refined nature and its beings were bright sparks like living stars. These beings could not get on together, however, caring only for their own brilliance. They could not reproduce themselves and neither cared nor felt a need to sing the praises of their creators. The Gods looked at their world and found it inadequate, so they destroyed it by turning its own nature against it. Fire rained down upon the world and it was consumed. The only survivors were the jaguars, for more than any

other creature they partook of that creation's fiery naure.

Meeting again, the Gods discussed the making of a world in much greater detail. Perhaps we need a world that is all mind, they said. After much planning they created the second sun, the world of mind. This attempt wasn't successful either, for everything moved too fast in a world of thought. No sooner did a thing come into being than it disappeared again. Nothing could manifest itself, for there was no time, and the world's transient beings were gone before they could reproduce or sing their creators' praises. The Gods saw that this world was no more than a world of air, which couldn't be grasped or held, and decided to destroy it as well with its own nature. They let the air tear it to pieces and the second sun was demolished with wind that rose in great gales and tore up the earth. The only survivors were the birds, for they had learned to move upon the winds.

The Gods then decided that their worlds lacked sensitivity. Let us make a world that is pure

feeling, they told themselves, so that all the creatures of it will love us and sing our praises. The third world was a beautiful watery world of perpetual rain, in which all was liquid and everything moved with great ponderousness. But the creatures here became completely involved with one another, moving in and out of each other with sultry flowings. The Gods quickly saw their error and let the waters flow faster and faster until everything was drowned. Only the fish survived, for they had learned to live in the water.

In creating a fourth world, the Gods decided to make a world so solid and dense that it could not flow like the waters, could not be so unstable as fire and air. The fourth world was made of pure action, which seemed to work until it was discovered that its creatures were too destructive. They did not get on well together for they crashed into each other with

An engraving on a bone found at Tikal, showing the five creatures of the five different creations on their journey through experience, which is depicted as a canoe with youth and vitality in front and wisdom and craft in the rear.

great force, until at last the earth rose up and buried everything. Because they are so agile, only the monkeys survived the fourth creation.

In darkness the creators met once again. They meditated upon their four failures and determined that their fifth world must be perfect. It would partake of all the previous worlds, would have a balanced proportion of the four elements, and would be the home of a comppletely new type of being.

It became clear to the Gods that when the earth was made and dawn flushed the sky, then man would appear and praise them. He would be given a voice and would be able to call their names in awe and gratitude. He would be able to name them one by one, calling on Feathered Serpent, Wind of Heaven, Heart of the Mountain, Heart of the Earth, Lightning Flash, Rolling Thunder, Smoking Mirror, No

Skin, and Grandfather, for these were the names of the nine Gods who gathered in the darkness and made the earth for man to walk upon. They made it well, also creating the light of day so that it could be a home for the thirteen gods who would inhabit the light.

The Gods looked at the fifth world and thought it was a good work. It will endure, they said, and amuse us for a long time. But when they looked at it again, they decided it was rather dull. It was static and lacked in excitement. It just sits there, they said. The creatures cannot grow for they have no challenge, no vitality. One of us will have to throw himself into this sun so that our god-energy gives the whole creation movement.

The question now was who would sacrifice himself for the amusement of all the others. No one seemed keen on the idea of destroying

himself, but finally Smoking Mirror (Tezcatlipoca) said: "I'm not afraid. I will make the sacrifice. That will make it a spectacular creation, and none of the Gods will ever forget me."

Smoking Mirror made offerings of beautiful Quetzal feathers and the rarest of incenses. He sang a hymn of praise for all of the Gods, who in turn praised him and paid honor to his strength and valor. But when it came right down to it, Smoking Mirror did not want to die. To see what would happen, he tested the sun by putting one foot slowly and carefully into it. The foot was instantly vaporized. He drew back immediately and would not go through with his decision. The other Gods certainly didn't blame him, so they replaced his missing foot with a mirror of obsidian, a smoky black volcanic glass, and in this mirror it is said he searches the fifth sun to find his foot.

Now that Smoking Mirror had recanted, what would the Gods do? None of them wanted to die, and as they discussed the problem a small voice from the very back of heaven spoke out: "I'll do it! Although I am very poor and have only meager offerings to make, I'll throw myself into the sun."

It was Xipe Totec, No Skin, who spoke up so bravely. He was the ugliest of all the Gods, for he was born without a skin and his flesh hung to his bones in revolting, smelly lumps. Being the poorest of the Gods, No Skin felt he had nothing to lose, so he made his tiny offering of the few things that he owned and threw himself into the sun.

The movement began. Everything began to turn—the planets began to go around the sun, and the satellites of the planets began to move around their mother bodies. The Gods looked on it and decided it was a wonderful, truly marvelous creation that would amuse them forever. They were most grateful to Xipe Totec, the Skinless One.

Then a miracle happened, for none of the Gods knew that there was a reward for the sacrifice. Xipe Totec was reborn as the God of Spring, since by his action in making movement he had quite accidentally invented time. All cyclical events are an expression of his sacrifice. He became the god of flowers, for they are the sign of spring and announce to the man-animal the need for sacrifice if life is to be sustained, the need to praise the Gods as they deserve to be praised.

This is a beautiful world, the Gods said, but we must never forget that it is made of the four previous worlds of spirit, mind, emotion and action. It is the man-animal's work to hold the four previous suns together within himself in a balanced manner: the fire of spirit, the air of the mind, the water of the emotions, and the material of the earth. Whenever this creature gets out of balance he will forget to sing the praises of the creator gods; and when he forgets to love us he will be destroyed by that very thing that has become unbalanced within

his nature, for this wonderful creation, like all of the others, carries within it the seed of its own destruction.

The jaguars survived the destruction of the world of spirit, the birds survived the world of pure mind, the fish survived the watery world of the emotions, and the monkeys survived the world of pure physical manifestation. The creatures who will survive the world of movement, this fifth sun, are those who maintain harmony and balance, and it is they who will inhabit the sixth sun that the gods call consciousness. The animal on that world will be the Hu-Man being, the divine-animal.

Men watched the cyclical movement of everything and they struggled very hard to understand it. They learned to count, progressing from one sun and moon to a thousand suns and more. The more they counted, the more they had to remember, and the task became arduous. They invented writings, made pictures which could stand for many things, and produced books. Gradually they recorded everything that happened, every star that moved, every seed that grew, every animal that swam or crawled or flew. They named each little part of everything they could see, even gave names to things they could not see.

The man-animal looked at everything and said, we will not die when this creation comes to an end. All the creatures of the previous creations were fools. We will not go down with this creation; we will understand what it is the gods are doing and we will defeat the gods. Not all of the creatures felt like this, however. There were those among them who said, you cannot defeat the gods, you cannot even understand the gods. You pretend that the gods are not here, yet it changes nothing. All that you do is imitate the gods; you cannot *be* one. You can make a chair, but you must make it out of wood and you cannot make the wood, much less make it out of nothing.

The creation of the fifth sun is always divided,

for those men who wish to defeat the gods are balanced by those who wish only to sing the praises of the gods and do the work of holding the creation in balance within themselves. There will always, be those who seek to hold the spirit, the mind, the emotions and the body together in a unity of balance and praise. When out of balance, they know they are vulnerable and can easily be destroyed by the very thing that is creating the imbalance.

Movement will wear out this sun, will destroy it. The earth will shake, the volcanoes will move the sea, and everything will come into conflict. By movement the fifth sun will end.

The ancient Mayas thought that the earth had its beginning in the year 3113 B.C., and that this creation of movement will have its ending on the twenty-first of December, 2011 A.D., amid terrible earthquakes, movement of the poles, volcanic activity, great tidal waves and terrible winds. All this will bring the fifth sun, the sun of man, to an end.

The Mayas believed that most of the destruction will take place between December 21st, 2011, and June 6th, 2012. The June date is very interesting because a rare planetary phenomenon occurs on that day. On an irregular but calculable course, the planet Venus will pass between the Earth and the sun, when it will be seen as a black dot on the face of the sun. The next transit will occur on June 8th, 2004, and last only a short while as it passes somewhat low on the disk; but on June 6th, 2012, the transit will last about eight hours as Venus will track across the widest area of the sun, dead center. (The last time the phenomenon was observed was in 1882 and lasted only several minutes.)

This sign from the planet Venus will usher in the new sun, the sixth creation, known by the Mayas as consciousness. Not a bad description of astrology's age of Aquarius, is it?

All good priests (scientists, teachers, thinkers) who serve the people never tire of pointing out that although the movement within the fifth sun was made by Our Lord the Skinless One, the creation also has in it the influence of the most powerful god in the pantheon, Our Lord Smoking Mirror. The creation was set in motion by the conflict between these two elements—a weak but open and loving force, freely given, and a dominant, powerful force that is being continually withdrawn.

Mankind has many talents, not least among them a talent for evil. Evil is called exploitation and mindlessness and is the sign of Our Lord Smoking Mirror, who is forever locked in rivalry with Our Lord Feathered Serpent, who represents love and understanding.

The Indian peoples expect the coming of Feathered Serpent any day now, and it is said that only when the feathered serpent has learned to fly will the sixth sun dawn. In Xultun Tarot he is thus depicted with wings, signifying that realization is a thing unique to each person, a movement that leaves no marks, no track which may be followed. It moves

through an element like air, where no footprints are left and no trail visible. It signifies a way that is unique and alone. Not lonely, but alone.

Pride has always been the downfall of human institutions. Pride isolates and makes an adequate response to "what is" quite impossible. The present creation owes its nature to the humblest of all the gods, who works quietly with the contribution of Lord Smoking Mirror. It is not a question of choosing The Skinless One over Smoking Mirror, but of finding a way in which each may contribute to the integrity and balance of our common good. They are both a part of the creation, and no good is served by ignoring one in favor of the other.

THE YEAR BEARER CEREMONY from the Dresden Codex. These four pages cover thirteen 52-year cycles. On the left of each page are repeated thirteen times the last day of one year and the first of the following year. The top pictures are priests wearing animal masks and tails, impersonating the bearers and carrying the burden of the different gods in charge of that time period. They are Rain, Jaguar, Maize and Death. In three bottom pictures the gods are casting grains of maize in a divination ritual (drawn after Gates copy).

The Yaqui Sorcerers And

Yaqui—vinaq, ahqixb ahcahb.

Among the Yaqui people—priests and sorcerers were many.

U kabavil Yaqui vinaq
Quetzalcoatl u bi.

The God of the Yaqui people also was Feathered Serpent.

—from Popol Vuh

The Yaqui Indians are often thought to be a rather late tribe, living somewhere near the border between the United States and Mexico. Yet the word Yaqui appears eight times in the Popol Vuh, or Book of Counsel, which was written soon after the Spanish conquest of the Mayas in Guatemala.

There are terrible tales of the Yaqui Indians who were hunted like animals by both Mexicans and Americans. Don Juan Matus, a Yaqui Sorcerer who twenty years ago took the young student Carlos Castaneda as a pupil, tells of the death of his mother as she was hunted down and killed by soldiers on horseback. There has been

a great deal of speculation as to whether Don Juan Matus actually lives or whether he is a character out of the imagination of Dr. Castaneda. Since it is the opinion of this writer that all writing is fiction, regardless of whether it is called history or romance or science—each book is rewritten by the person who reads it, and we each make our own understanding out of what is between the covers—a discussion of the 'reality' of Don Juan will have little purpose. That there are parallels between what the Yaqui teacher says and the little that remains to us of the religious thought of the Mayas, there can be no doubt at all, and we will proceed to examine these teachings in the light of the Mayan tarot.

The Sorcerer's power is unimaginable, and the extent to which a student may understand it is governed among other things by the degree of the commitment to it. The full use of the power can only be accomplished by the use of an "ally," a kind of spirit guide, who is not altogether benevolent and who challenges the student when the student is able to "see."

The Maya view of reality (a concept shared by almost all native American groups) clearly defines existence as having two parts, the TONAL and the NAGUAL.

The Tonal is the world of Form, the world order that is made by the mind. Each person has a view of existence, and each believes this view to be complete. A moment's reflection will show that it is not complete at all. The illusion of completeness comes because of consciousness, which is the content of mind itself. Although the mind may see mysterious things, it cannot explain them. To explain them would be to lose the mystery, so what is mysterious remains so and does not enter the realm of the known. Consequently the mind is never aware of any gaps in its "seeing." The great Mystery, the experiencable unknown, is called the Nagual. It cannot be explained, discussed, or brought into the field of consciousness.

There are five basic movements (or paths) through the Tonal, which give the Sorcerer access to the Nagual. They are not separate

Their View of Reality.

steps but more like accomplishments, and are generally worked on all at the same time, though at different times certain aspects assume more importance than others. For the sake of clarity we will examine them one at a time and relate them to the higher arcana of the tarot.

The first movement is called ERASING PERSONAL HISTORY, which refers to the moment within the mind and is admirably demonstrated within the Priestess card. Seated between the black pillar and the white pillar, the card displays the method by which the mind stores information—in opposites. When the mind forms, grasps, and understands a concept, it generally does so by first seeing the negative aspect (we don't know what love is, but we sure can know what it isn't!), followed by its opposite, by which a concept is born. Most persons grasp and store concepts, not from direct seeing but from (so-called) education. They learn and recall concepts, so the basic movement is like and dislike, pleasure and pain, right and wrong. The "I" is born quickly, and

it is always thought of as the "good," the "positive." People do not think of themselves as negative, disruptive, ugly, bad, violent, or unworthy; these qualities always belong to another. Ask anyone what sort of person they are and they will tell you in lurid and wondrous detail, a great list of likes and dislikes. Try this on yourself. State who you are without saying what you do—that is, don't say "I'm a carpenter" or "I'm a housewife"—and notice how difficult it is to answer the question with this one restriction, for you immediately must enter the mystery of your existence.

We live in a terribly dangerous world, and much of the threat comes from categorizing ourselves with labels: religious, political, national, and sexist. The identification of the "I" is always an illusion, but so powerful an illusion that people will kill and die for it.

No matter how strong an illusion is, it remains an illusion and can never truly be reality. A bit of history may help clarify this concept.

The great astronomer Galileo Galilei observed that when the chandelier in the cathedral moved, it would swing in an arc that had a distinct rhythm. He timed this movement with his pulse. Galileo did not create something but observed a law of motion in action and was able to formulate it mathematically. The result of the "seeing" was the pendulum, as well as the use of the observed principal in a device to measure the pulse beat of a person. The "seeing" took place because Galileo was able to put himself and what he knew aside. Later, when he formulated the 'law of falling bodies,' he encountered great opposition, even though he did a very famous public experiment by letting a one-pound ball and a ten-pound ball fall simultaneously from the tower of Pisa. Both balls hit the ground at the same time, yet Galileo was fired from his job and experienced great trouble, since everyone *knew* the law of Aristotle which said the ten-pound ball would fall ten times faster than the one-pound ball (they knew it but never tested it).

The ego believes what it wants to believe and

accepts the "authority" that backs it up. The ego is lazy. Work is dangerous to it, observation is dangerous to it, for it is a house built upon sand and will brook no inspection of foundations that may be quite insecure.

Memory, the attribute of the Priestess card, makes the accretion of the "I" possible. What can one do—erase memory? Then you would never be able to find your way home, or even speak. Galileo absent-mindedly watched a swinging chandelier and his intelligence observed an order of motion which then became part of his mind's "order." Galileo was able to verbalize the experience, at least in mathematics, but not immediately. Could he say "I understand" or "understanding took place?" Could he ever honestly say, other than speculatively, "I will understand!" Hasn't understanding always *just* happened? Hasn't seeing always *just* taken place? Hasn't the lightning always *just* struck, no matter what we may think or do about it afterward? When one knows something—does it have to be remembered—or is it part of consciousness for life!

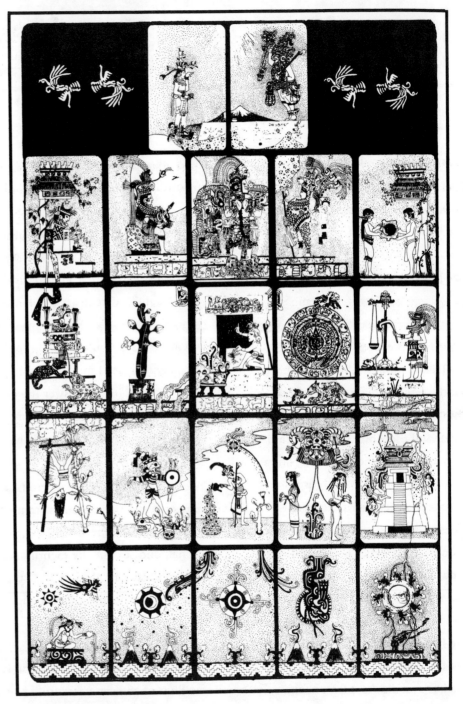

THE ASSEMBLED HIGHER ARCANA OF THE XULTUN TAROT DECK.

The card below the Priestess is the Warrior card, and its attribute is speech. Inextricably interwoven with memory, speech is indeed an extension of memory, just as the wheel is an extension of the leg or the telescope an extension of the eye. Remembering is an action that takes place in the now; what is remembered is always the past. The words used and the ideas expressed with those words are always from the past. "What a beautiful sunset!"—the words are learned in the past, and the idea of beauty is a concept formed at some past observation of a sunset, which is being recalled and compared with the sunset that is occurring in the now. The words (speech) have trapped the speaker in the past. A person deaf from birth, never having heard a word connected to a thing, and perhaps having no concept of speech, still sees the sunset. The person has no word for it, yet recognizes the event and still compares it with other sunsets. The student sorcerer will eventually see how the mind labels a natural phenomenon and then measures the label, ignoring the actual happening. Mankind's culture serves to reinforce the cul-ture until it become buried in absurdities and the individual can no longer function.

The Warrior does battle with speech, always on the alert, always aware, suspicious of every verb, cautious of every noun. He watches his words and slashes out at implications, listens to no authority, heeds no commander. The Warrior observes the miraculous character of everyday events. His terrain is the world within. Note the two jaguars, how alert and attentive they are. They are black and white, and they are not free. The jaguars are tied to the Warrior's chair (representing his conceptual world under control), free to attack when required but limited to the Warrior's bidding. The Warrior's world is not a world limited to introspection, for it is a world of action. This world of here and now is the Warrior's hunting ground.

The next card in the path of Erasing Personal History is the Hanged Man. It represents the mind itself, the mind brought to its very limit, brought to that place where it reflects back on itself like a corridor of mirrors. It is the limitation of the mind, the place where it reflects the method by which it has constructed itself, the place where the mind's habitual way of acting without limits comes up flat against limits. It represents the barrier, the skin, the unbridgeable void between the picture of reality that the mind has made and the inexplicable world of reality. The dead tree, the hangman's tree, is the past, the known world; the living tree, is the inexplicable mystery of now. One cannot be taken into the other. There is a radiation from the body of the Hanged Man, for this is a holy position. The body has never forsaken the now, it *is* the now. It never deals with the past. This card demonstrates how deep the division between the body and the mind can become.

The last card in the process of Erasing Personal History is called the Star. It is traditionally given the value of 'meditation.' It is the functioning of the process of awareness without choice that erases personal history, an action that comes about in a negative manner. The Warrior's point of observation is the sword that continually cuts down the world of the mind, the world of the known. Meditation is an opening-up process, an alertness grounded in total freedom, which is the only way that one may free one's self from the tyranny of what is believed to be known. What you think you know is your personal history.

The next path to examine is called DEATH THE ADVISOR. In this process, not separate from the first process but running parallel to it, the would-be sorcerer discovers the wholeness of existence and the interdependence of all life movement.

The top card is the Consort, and its value is reaction, the process of movement between opposites. Clinging to life is a movement based in fear of death, and fear of death is based in a belief that life is not supporting one. The entire movement is a reaction that has its energy in the concept that death is an end of life, not that death is a part of life. Our society thinks it is absolutely natural to do anything and everything possible to stay the hand of the Grim Reaper. To conceive of death as a friend is quite alien to the Western mind. To hold one's death clearly in one's mind in a tender and loving manner is considered by most Western thinkers as perverse and akin to insanity. (Oh, it is possibly all right for saints and poets, even perhaps for a few philosophers who deal strictly in ideas, to propose the concept, but they are not to be taken seriously.) His death is the Sorcerer's only true friend, for it keeps the Warrior in him at attention and brings about an order that is based in reality. Death instills a spirit of conservation and clear-seeing seriousness. The Sorcerer is serious about everything, and Death is a serious friend who will not be denied at any price. Death awaits each one of us, and no amount of fear, illusion, or flight will change that. In the end we all accept. (A study regarding the victims of capital punishment showed an interesting fact—no person has been carried screaming into the gas chamber. Each went passively and quietly, accepting the inevitable.)

The card below the Consort is the Cactus, the card of endurance. Death teaches endurance, not patience. It teaches a passive strength, the ability to 'hang in there.' Patience requires will power. Endurance is not based in the will but in interaction with what is occurring, as long as it is occurring. Endurance has its strength in inevitability and in freedom.

The next card down is the Death card. It does not refer only to physical death but also to psychological death, the dying that must take place to every concept, to every idea that holds us, and which prevents the flowering of freedom within the whole being. The Sorcerer must have the freedom to enquire, otherwise he can never arrive at the goal of entering the Nagual. Fear of death prevents one from living and makes a virtue out of monotonous, risk-free existence, makes a virtue out of boredom, and makes illusion preferable to reality.

The last card is the Moon. This card calls us to observe sleep. Sleep is often called the "little death," and not without reason; yet people afraid of death look forward to sleep and call

The hieroglyph for movement, *the sign of this present cycle. At the center is a cactus with two knives buried in it; represented in this manner the sign means penitence.   (After a design from Teotihuacan.)*

it the great blessing, which seems strange. Perhaps not, however, for if one has never been truly awake, how can sleep assume any significance? What happens to the "I" when we sleep? Does it sleep too, or does it just stop being? Sleep is the embrace of our loving friend Death. When we realize that each action may be our last, when we are not lulled to sleep by habit, when we are alone and death is the very root of our life, only then can one's actions become impeccable, only then is one totally at union with one's environment and unencumbered by the baggage of what one knows.

STOPPING THE WORLD is the next path laid out in the cards. The top card is the card of action called the Ruler. The objective is to disrupt the illusion harbored in the mind of a continuum of events, which makes action impossible and leaves us continually reacting to things we believe happen to us. Stopping the process of judgment and categorization is an arduous task and must enlist the aid of the body. The first concern must be ourselves. If I do not love myself, how can I love my neighbor? If I am continually keeping the body dulled with tobacco and other drugs, it means that the body and "I" are not acquainted at all.

The mind in its relationship with the body is comparable to a rich man living in a beautiful house, behind which is an overgrown yard where he keeps several savage, half-starved dogs. Every now and then, when he remembers, he opens a window and throws a few chunks of meat to the dogs. This has been going on for many years and he wishes it were different, but he's afraid to go down among the dogs.

When neither the mind nor the body has set itself up as master, then action can take place, and the Sage card expresses this through the attribute of touch. Touch is the body's awareness. The body's observations do not take place within the mind, although that is the place where all of the data is stored. Observation takes place all over the body, through the use of *all* the senses, of which touch is the most proscribed. This proscription of touch limits our society and relegates it squarely within the confines of mind, consequently no action is possible, only reaction.

The Temperance card presents the reward and the method. A life brought into harmony is its own reward. The "bringing" cannot be done by the mind and cannot be based in an idea, regardless of how "logical" the idea may seem. Harmony is brought into a life by action, and there is no amount of scheming or planning that can bring it about. Action is not connected to a cause. Action is.

The Sun is the last card and represents total

energy. When the mind ceases its games of control and harmony is restored to the being, there is brought about a great change in personality. The past is dead; it no longer blocks and channels energy to bring about the mind's wishes. Energy flows freely to wherever it is needed, at the time it is needed. The body responds with its wisdom and gives freely all of the information available to it. The world of the mind has been stopped and untold benefits of energy are available to be used as creative force (to enter the Nagual).

The next path is called THE DREAMER AND THE KNOWING and deals with the actual world that we inhabit, the world of time with its laws of nature and reciprocal events.

    Am I a butterfly dreaming I am a man,
    Or am I a man dreaming I am a butterfly?

It also deals with the cultural perceptions that are the form and order mankind has made out of observation of the world of nature.

The top card is the Priest. This card has the value of tradition and as such it is the card of the teacher, the master, or guru. It represents the one who points the way. Tradition by its very nature is blind to now. Tradition as a moral law can only be immoral. It is not necessary to condemn tradition, for love will set us free of it. All we need do is understand it, we need not look to it for guidance. The Priest, or teacher, must pass on the teachings, and the student is then bound, first to understand and then to set himself free of them. The pupil is free only when he has discovered the teaching for himself, which is the liberating factor, for then the teachings are part of the student, and set him free of the past. The adversary of the teacher and the culture is the student who learns by rote. This is the immoral factor in tradition, for repetition is the murder of the mind. The modern system of education is a pathetic shadow of teaching, quite contrary to its stated aims and ideals. The word 'education' means to lead out that which is latent.

The Wheel card is next in line and is dedicated to learning. That is the card of law, that is, all cyclical events—the eternal return of the seasons, the wondrous cycle from seed to fruit. It also governs more obscure laws such as gravity, the law of falling bodies, and the law of entropy (diminishing returns of energy). The lesson of the Wheel is openness, for learning takes place when the whole business of "knowing" is put aside.

Next is the Bound Man, and its value is mirth. Laughter is the only way that the bondage of learning may be broken. The pompous teacher, repository of outmoded traditional hogwash (such as Aristotle's never-observed law of falling bodies), can only be demolished with laughter. Mirth cleanses the mind of its crazy cobweb designs, leaving space for nurturing to take place. This open space within the mind must always be free, so that ideas and realties can be observed and allowed to find their own level, or eventually dissipate.

The last card is the Planet Venus. This is the card of awareness, the result of the watchful openness of the student. This is what is left when everything has, in freedom, found its level. Awareness is the jewel of the warrior, the heart of the creative person. The real world is seen only through awareness, which sweeps aside the cobwebs of "reason" and makes the law visible.

The last column displays the path called AS-SUMING AUTHORITY, and it is this final movement that crowns the achievement of the Sorcerer. The Sorcerer assumes total authority for the world. He has made it and is responsible for it, and nothing happens that is not his invention. He does not assume his authoirty as a conscious decision; quite the contrary, the authority is his because he acts. He does not choose authority; it is wholly contained within any action the Sorcerer engages in. Because there is no divison within the Sorcerer, all of his actions are positive and not related to choice. The actions come about because they are the thing to do at that time.

Most of us, by our education at school and our conditioning in the world, have learned to ask questions, usually to demonstrate that we are interested or to show we are sympathetic. The Sorcerer searches out the question, since the right question will illuminate the problem and display the answer. Therefore an answer from outside will be unnecessary. Most of us ask questions as a reaction and await an answer from somewhere . . . anywhere.

The top card is the Lovers, and it is the card that is given the value of the sense of smell, which displays to us that the real world does not stop where we can see it. All matter is inter-penetrating, that is, it fills up all space. The table does not stop at the surface, and neither does the rose. The lesson of authority is once more the lesson of oneness. This theme is continually backed up by the senses no matter where we look. The Lovers card shows how everything must be allowed to find its balance, without interference.

The next card is Balance, the card of decision. The creative person is involved equally with destruction and the movements within crea-tion, and destruction, decision, and need must be examined. The real world will brook no decision by man, but within the artificial world of human culture (the word 'art' means arti-ficial), decisions are rife. Man decided to build the hydrogen bomb, to educate in a certain manner, and such decisions are shaped and molded by the "seeing" of each individual. If the seeing is confused, it is because the in-dividual is confused, and confused individuals make a confused society.

The tarot is a decision—a commitment, if you will. It is a decision to put a foot on the path of righteousness, to hear no authority but to assume it. It is a decision to investigate with openness and integrity, and to the best of one's ability, everything that speaks to the mind and body. Judge not, for judgments are based in prejudice and cut at the openness of the mind in its investigation of "what is."

The lightning of decision strikes the temple in the card called the Lightning-Struck Tower.

The decision arrived at in total freedom releases one from all structures of knowledge built up by the mind, releases one from all attachment. The decision is as free as lightning, and no one commands the lightning. It is only when one is cast out of the house of knowledge that integrity comes into being.

The Planet Earth card demonstrates the integrity, unity, and oneness that we have been searching for. Only in the moment of least expectation does it happen. As the Bible phrases it, "like a thief in the night, shall it come."

The Sorcerer is born when the fool ceases to be foolish. Integrity comes when one ceases to be separate. None of this may come about as an act of will, and there is nothing we may do to arrive at understanding, for understanding is an accident. The most we can do is become accident prone.

The Mayas left us the ruins of an enigmatic civilization. It is obvious that they valued its outside trappings only passingly; yet as a people they still survive, independent, democratic in their institutions, firm, honest, valuing and making few demands upon one another.

Long ago the native American population discovered how to live in harmony with life, and we are beginning to see that our transplanted European civilization does not do this well. We can look to the original Americans and observe their ways. We can openly examine the order they saw, the order that is a result of the Great Spirit of this land. We cannot lose by this examination. We may even find that inner peace we so desperately seek and that has so willfully eluded us.

The Western civilizations have not produced a great teacher. Joshua Bar Joseph, the Christ, was a Semite of the Jewish persuasion and sought only to reform the Jewish church. He did not start a new religion, although one was begun in his name. Abdul Muhammed, another Semite, was the founder and prophet of Islam.

All the world's teachers have been from the far and near east. Perhaps the Americas will see another incarnation of Feathered Serpent. The Mayas say the time is ripe and the Hopi people expect the teacher daily. Perhaps then a moral basis for life will become apparent to us. Perhaps then we will see an end to the divisions that rend our society.

FEATHERED SERPENT AS LORD OF THE DAWNING.

This drawing is taken from a late Toltec work and has been translated so to speak into an image that with a little explanation can be understood by those not so familiar with Maya iconography.

Feathered Serpent is pictured as the Planet Venus when it rises ahead of the sun as the morning star, his face looks out the mouth of the serpent. The scales about the eyes and the Fangs make the butterflies' wings that are the symbol of realization. The Venus sign above the mouth is the "mouth" through which the Sun is born each morning, the bottom one forming the tongue of the serpent is the "mouth" that swallows the sun at night; both together show the path of the sun through the underworld. The large squares show the Tonal and the Nagual, the divine opposites which are magically created, for when only one line is drawn the two come about together.

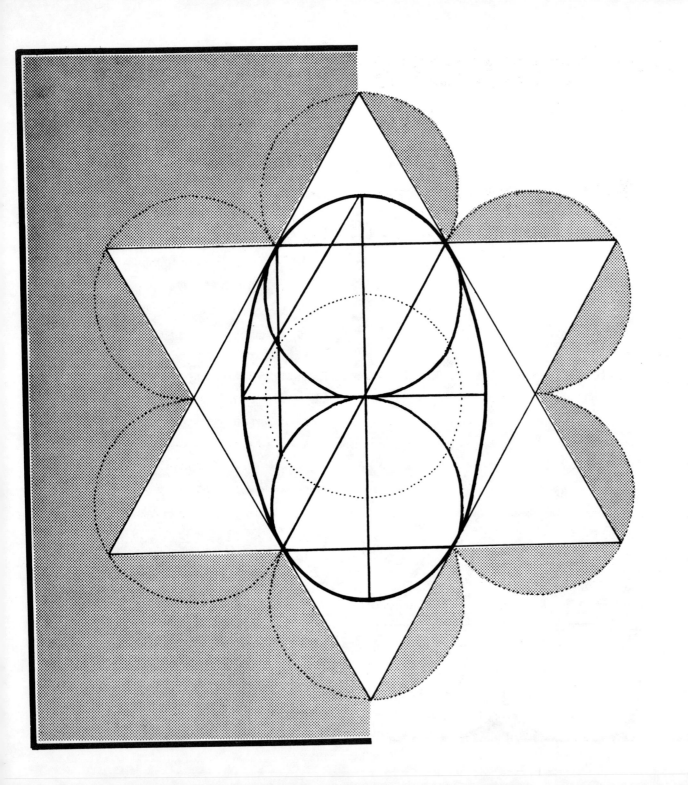

The Hidde

The Mayas were among the most sophisticated of people when it came to mathematics, and there is no doubt at all that they incorporated this knowledge into a complex system of what we would today call numerology. The Western world has a way of dividing knowledge into categories and then dismissing them, but the Mayas took an entirely different view. Astronomy was the key to astrology, the key to its interpretation and categorization. Indeed, astronomers today still use the ancient astrological division of the sky to provide the base upon which knowledge of the heavens is drawn.

Numbers were expressed in precisely the same way. What we consider as one of the great intellectual triumphs of the Maya people was the establishing of the concept of zero. It's hard for us to imagine just how difficult it is to formulate the idea that nothing can be represented as something. We take it for granted, but if we think about it, it becomes mind boggling. This concept seems to be fundamental to all native American thinking. The Nagual, the unknown part of creation that can

Meaning of Numbers in the Tarot.

never be brought into manifestation yet can be experienced, can be sensed and known, but in a different way, a way that cannot be translated, cannot be transplanted, expressed in words or the form of our everyday images is as real as a tree and just as inexplicable. A tree may be explained eventually in numbers, reduced to a series of mechanical responses, yet there is a totally mysterious part that cannot ever be explained. The life within a tree, that expresses itself through a tree, cannot be explained with mechanics.

To the Maya numbers were a way of expressing that which could not be expressed in any other terms, for numbers embodied the very mysteries of the universe itself. A 'trip mechanism' was needed, something that could overshoot the world of limitation and form, and for them numbers did this. The whole cosmology was expressed through numbers and entire orders of priests were devoted to the study, observation, and use of numbers.

(0) Zero expressed the great unknown, the mystery of why things lived and continued on their path in order and virtue, the Nagual.

(1) The Creator, the god of creation called Tzacol. Like all Maya gods, this is an expression, not a person. Tzacol is considered the supernatural source of energy, which is thought to be monolithic and freely available to all, not separate expressions of energy but one energy used to the extent of individual ability. The Mayas felt that after the initial energy flow, nothing could be created or destroyed, it could only be changed. The Mayas expressed one in symbol as a dot or point (•) and by a simple change of its position it could express a value from one to infinite.

(2) The duality of expression in form and matter, the one giving birth to its opposite, the compliment and the dissident. This concept is expressed as Feathered Serpent (Kukulcan), the spiritual, the highest

aspects combined within the body of the lower aspects, the snake and the bird. All creation that humankind is involved with expresses itself through this dualism; indeed it is this dualism which gives creation its energy.

(3) The formulator god was called Bitol, the "molder" of the clay of creation. Bitol was an expression of the rule by which energy and duality caused change to express itself in ever-varying and complex patterns of creation. The "molder" was the means by which change expressed itself and took on form that was a suitable expression for the work to which a living entity directed itself.

(4) The square of creation, the rich and limitless world of form as expressed in material, Alom, the Earth mother goddess, the source and supply of all our needs. The symbol for Alom is a flower with four petals. She is the Earth that receives the corn, is blessed with the fecundating rays of the Father Sun, and who gives a thousandfold in return for love and respect.

(5) Cajalon is the male creative element, the father of life. The Sun at its zenith, shedding its energy for all, creating and destroying in an eternal pulsing rhythm, burning with equity and justice. Cajalon is life itself within any of its manifestations. The form of Cajalon is expressed in the rise of a pyramid from the base to its peak, the four corners and the center.

(6) The beauty of divine expression is called the Governor, Tepeu. It was Tepeu who put order into the furthest reaches of creation. The Governor Tepeu is the movement towards the complimentary expression of divergent parts, the virtue which is heard in differing modes. This aspect is expressed in two groups of three, three parts above and three parts below (:·:), synthesis and antithesis.

(7) The Heart of the Mountain. The victorious expression of a life which has its base in the unfailing wisdom of life as it emanates from its primal source. This number has the quality of standing alone and does not go into any other. It is the unique unresolving quality within all nature.

(8) This number is the expression of confidence in the eternal splendor of the creation, as it is expressed in all of life. This confidence enables us to be "at home" with nature, not seeking to dominate it. It bestows the peace of understanding.

(9) This number can be expressed as three groups of three. Three above, three below, and three in harmony—or thought, word, and deed. It imparts the sure knowledge that one's life rests each day, each hour, each second upon the sure foundation of Divine Love, whose selfless self-fulfilling purpose, incomprehensible to us, still supports us.

(10) The complete inseparable, non-combining Nagual and Tonal. The wholeness and unity within their complete mutual support of each other. There is not and never can be separation between the one and the whole, as there may not ever be union either.

Numbers as the Maya see them are the extreme reduction of philosophic thought and should not be considered as mere "enumeraton." The first nine numbers are considered the nine-hour "Gods" of night, and they are primary, for all was darkness upon the face of all creation, which was not. The Gods met in darkness and created the cosmos. From darkness came light. The prime numbers are all entitites that are made up of units, 3 being one unit of three units, the two previous units (the opposites) and conciliation. Upon examination you will see that all the numbers are expressed in this manner. This is also true of their numerical expression in mathematics—for example, the number 4 is the value that determines forms. It has the quality of determining the equality of the surface and circumference of a circle or a square. A square whose side is FOUR measures SIXTEEN in circumference and SIXTEEN in surface. A circle whose diameter is FOUR measures 4π in circumferrence and 4π in surface.

It is the consideration of the function of numbers that gives them their philosophical value. The ancient people referred to this as the "science of numbers," and it operated constantly in all aspects of their lives. The number of the day determined the height of the proposed construction; the day of birth told all about the life that was to be lived.

*This is a drawing of a superb glyph on a commemorative tablet of stone found in the city of Palenque. It is part of a calendar inscription and it says, **no days**, that is; so many years, so many months and no days. Depicted is a young man with one of the markings for zero on his arm supporting an old man who is weak and dying. This exquisite contrast between the young and the old, and the beauty in both figures, points to the sensitivity these people had towards numbers. The only other place where this type of glyph appears is Copan, the most Eastern of the Maya cities. Palenque is the most Western city, that should tell us something about them.*

The Twenty

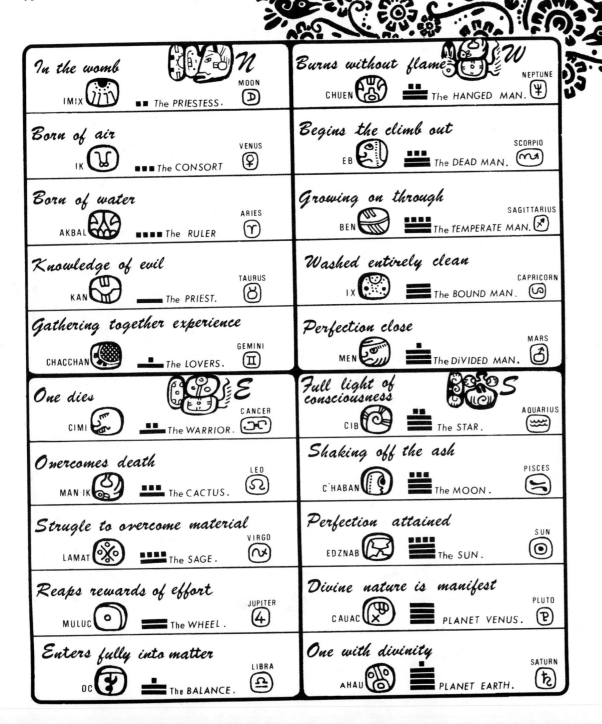

In the womb	IMIX ▪▪ The PRIESTESS.	MOON Ⓓ	
Born of air	IK ▪▪▪ The CONSORT	VENUS ♀	
Born of water	AKBAL ▪▪▪▪ The RULER	ARIES ♈	
Knowledge of evil	KAN ▬ The PRIEST.	TAURUS ♉	
Gathering together experience	CHACCHAN ▪ The LOVERS.	GEMINI ♊	
One dies	CIMI ▪▪ The WARRIOR.	CANCER ♋	
Overcomes death	MAN-IK ▪▪▪ The CACTUS.	LEO ♌	
Strugle to overcome material	LAMAT ▪▪▪▪ The SAGE.	VIRGO ♍	
Reaps rewards of effort	MULUC ▬ The WHEEL.	JUPITER ♃	
Enters fully into matter	OC ▪ The BALANCE.	LIBRA ♎	
Burns without flame	CHUEN ▬ The HANGED MAN.	NEPTUNE ♆	
Begins the climb out	EB ▬ The DEAD MAN.	SCORPIO ♏	
Growing on through	BEN ▬ The TEMPERATE MAN.	SAGITTARIUS ♐	
Washed entirely clean	IX ▬ The BOUND MAN.	CAPRICORN ♑	
Perfection close	MEN ▬ The DIVIDED MAN.	MARS ♂	
Full light of consciousness	CIB ▬ The STAR.	AQUARIUS ♒	
Shaking off the ash	C'HABAN ▪▪▪ The MOON.	PISCES ♓	
Perfection attained	EDZNAB ▪▪▪▪ The SUN.	SUN ☉	
Divine nature is manifest	CAUAC ▬ PLANET VENUS.	PLUTO ♇	
One with divinity	AHAU ▬ PLANET EARTH.	SATURN ♄	

The science of numbers was raised to unprecedented heights by the Maya. Their view of time was of great in-breathings and out-breathings of the cosmos, not of evolving but of changing, great cycles of time. This view meant that they saw history in terms of repetition that was extended over eons of time, and we have extant a Mayan inscription going back four hundred million years into the past. There are others that look ahead at least four thousand years into the future.

Most Central American peoples based their calendars on cycles of twenty-day periods arranged in multiples of eighteen, so that 20 x 18 equalled 360 days. To the 360 days were added five days that were considered outside the calendar, to form a complete year. The 365-day year was corrected so that the Maya were able to fix the true passage of the Earth about the Sun at 365.2420 days, which is only two ten-thousandths of a day short of our modern calculation which is 365.2422. The Gregorian calendar fixes the year at 365.2425 days, or three ten-thousandths of a day too long.

Day-Journeys of the Maya Month.

Modern science thinks this a remarkable accomplishment for a stone-age people. It is to be remembered that the Maya did not use metal until quite late in their development. For those who have an astronomical bent, I will continue with the Mayas' astounding abilities at combining observed phenomena and mathematical representation.

The agricultural or solar calendar of 365 days, multiplied by two 52-year periods, gives 37,960 days; 146 times the Holy calendar of 260 days also gives 37,960 days. The synodic revolutions of the planet Venus are 584 x 65, or 37,960 days. All this was arranged so that every 104 years these three calendars coincided.

And there is more. Five periods of 260 days make 1,300 days, or 44 revolutions of the moon around the Earth. The cycle of the planet Venus is 584 days, or 2.25 x 260. One cycle of Mars is 780 days, or exactly 3 x 260. The cycle of the planet Jupiter is 399 days, that is, almost 22 x 18. The cycle of Saturn is

378 days, or 360 + 18. This remarkable grouping of time into 9 hours of night, 13 hours of day, a 20-day month, and an 18-month year supplied them with all of the divisions and multiples needed to fix both the Sacred and the Profane rounds of the calendar in such a manner that, at what were considered very important days, all of the starting points coincided.

The Maya procession of days, or twenty-day journeys of the month, are not just as our calendar is, a way of telling one day from the other. It is much more. The twenty days are named after twenty steps to enlightenment, a continual reminder to the Indians of their primary duty. The Mayas understood the law of diminishing returns, that is, that more energy must be put into an operation than can be gotten out of it. A person is born and immediately upon partition begins to use the energy of the sun and the various plants and other forms of stored energy. When the person dies the energy returns to the common stockpile of mother Earth, but not all of it returns.

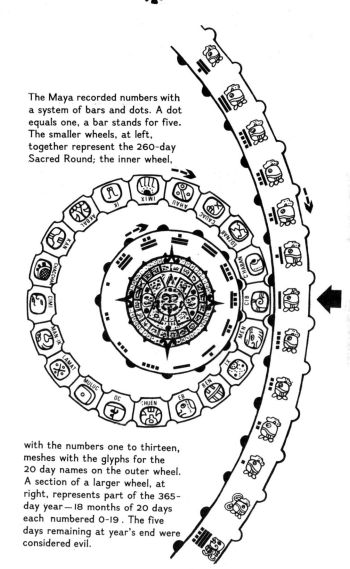

The Maya recorded numbers with a system of bars and dots. A dot equals one, a bar stands for five. The smaller wheels, at left, together represent the 260-day Sacred Round; the inner wheel,

with the numbers one to thirteen, meshes with the glyphs for the 20 day names on the outer wheel. A section of a larger wheel, at right, represents part of the 365-day year—18 months of 20 days each numbered 0-19. The five days remaining at year's end were considered evil.

Some is lost along the journey of life. The Mayas felt that only the realized person returned that energy, indeed multiplied it and returned it in great abundance. Unless persons strove for and achieved realization, the sun would eventually run down, all of its energy used up.

The diagram that accompanies this chapter shows how each of the twenty days is attached to a card of the higher arcana, making a very effective correlation between the two systems of thought. That such a system existed in ancient times, the writer has no doubt at all; unfortunately, along with Maya astrology, it has been lost. It is quite remarkable how very well the two systems do fit, however, this is not too surprising, since they are meant to do the same job, even though they are from different cultures.

The procession of days represents man's spiritual pilgrimage. They are twenty steps, not leading one to the other, one building upon the other until the final edifice of realization is created.

IMIX comes from the word IM, the womb. It in the womb of memory that the "I" is born. The individuation of the person has its start with remembrance.

IK, that is, spirit or breath (air), the Maya regarded as the primal nourishment, the first blessing of the Creator spirit, bestowed freely upon us.

AKBAL, born of water. The pre-Hispanic peoples practiced a baptism that was a replay of the first birth. It took place at about the age of twelve or thirteen and had many of the qualities of the modern "rebirth" experience. It wiped the slate clean, so to speak, allowing the person a new beginning, free of past conditioning.

KAN, he begins to know evil. This, the fourth step or hurdle, means he has knowledge and it must be overcome. All that the initiate knows is wrong and evil, and a way must be found to be free of it.

CHACCHAN. At the fifth hurdle, the candidate for enlightenment must gather together all experience, examine conditioning, see how it operates in the view of the Tonal.

CIMI. One dies to all that has been gathered. Only in death is there freedom from the known, and dying becomes a way of life. Only with death as a constant adviser are correct values given to the perception of existence.

MAN-IK. This step is named from MANZAL-IK, that is, to pass through the spirit. At this hurdle death is overcome, and the first manifestation of the death of the "I" is as a physical death. Having surrendered to the death of the body, the "I" is left without a host body and assumes its rightful place, no more the dominator of the organism but a completely equal partner, no more and no less important than any other part of the body.

LAMAT, whose sign is Venus, shows the candidate that the overcoming of knowledge gives power, and that power must be overcome, the material world must not engulf the person who has put a foot on the path.

MULUC. On this, the ninth day, one reeps the reward of all the effort expended. At this stage it is seen that all effort is wasted effort. Until now the person has made effort to avoid effort, a very contradictory way to act . . . so far.

OC. Now that the burden of the known has been shed and the view of the Tonal seen for what it is, the apprentice is free to enter fully into the state of things. The whole being is freed from the limitations of having a "view," and entry into matter takes place.

CHUEN, to burn without flame, is to suffer. A darkness of the soul overtakes the apprentice, and there is no way out. What went so well up to now seems all to no avail. All is silent; it seems the door is closed.

EB. On the twelfth day what is to be a long process begins, the climb out. It is represented as the growing of the maize plant. Until now the seed was only planted; now the growing begins. The seed is dying and with fructification is transformed into new life, the plant grows upward, utilizing the stored energy within the seed.

BEN. The death of the seed is the birth of the plant. The eternal return has begun, the growing is continuing, and the burden of the past becomes lighter.

IX. Washed entirely clean by the rains, the maize flourishes. The candidate is totally free of the past, the energy of the seed has gone, and the brink of the Nagual is approachable. No view holds the student back.

MEN. Although close to perfection, the apprentice is not yet there. No more is there a preoccupation with the process, for it is well under way. Only passion and tireless work can supply the energy needed.

CIB. The full light of consciousness is turned upon all of the Tonal. Everything is seen for what it is and no illusions remain, except one, which is consciousness itself.

C'HABAN. The light of consciousness, turned upon all perception, itself must go, burned to ash. Even that ash must be shaken off. Nothing may remain of the past if the next step is to be attained.

EDZNAB. Perfection attained. The apprentice has completed the task; the past is dead, all fear stilled, and death is perpetually cutting down all movement of the "I." Energy flows freely.

CAUAC. The divine nature is manifest in the Sorcerer. There are no obstructions, no impediments, no desires, no will, no choice.

AHAU. The circle is complete. The apprentice has reached the source, the Nagual, and is one with divinity. No separation is possible. The personality is a tool that can be used to create invisibility.

Sexual Expression and the Tarot:

At first glance it may appear rather difficult to connect the tarot with one's sexual expression, but there has always been the connection in traditional tarot. There simply has been a reluctance to talk about it. Sex has mostly been spoken of in terms such as 'does he love me?,' 'Will I be able to win her?,' and so on. Of course the fortune-telling aspects of the tarot have always dealt with the birth of children and the like.

If there is a lesson to be learned by our age, it seems to have to do with sex. Our society is a repressive one, at least from the point of individual liberty. There has been a long-standing belief (thought of as scientific) in Western society, that everyone is essentially the same, and nowhere has this prejudice been so strong as in the realm of sex. We are very fond of crowing about liberty, freedom of speech, etc. The writer suggests that if we look at those who have spoken out in favor of such freedoms, however, we will find that they mostly have been silenced, either with bullets or with prison.

Within our society there is a definite connection between sex, food, and money. We also hear a lot of talk about the PERMISSIVE SOCIETY, the implication being that society as a whole has relaxed its control over sex. The truth is that the relaxing of control has not come about because the society has become more understanding, but because of the complexity of the rules of control and the fact that it has never been easy to decide what was 'art' and what was 'pornography.'

In an examination of sex we must begin with the act itself. Is it as fundamental Christians believe, inherently evil? Is it the original sin? Looking around the planet we find that sex is almost the universal mode by which all species reproduce their kind. Next time you admire the beauty of a rose or enjoy the perfume of a flower, remember that flowers are the sex organs of plants. It is hard to believe that life is fundamentally evil. The writer totally rejects that view, feeling that all the evidence of senses points in the other direction.

Is the sex act a problem to overcome? Surely the act of sex is no more a problem than is eating or drinking. If we look carefully it will be seen that sex is not the problem—it is what we think about sex that makes the difficulty. If one thinks about sex all the time, one has a problem, no less than if one thinks about food all the time. If one gets no satisfaction from the sex act, one has a problem. If one is consumed with guilt because of the act, one has a problem. Perhaps it is now clear that the problem is not the act of sex but the thought about the act.

Somewhere early in our lives each one of us makes a decision about sex. We are not born heterosexual or homosexual, we are born sexual beings. We make a decision based upon our view of this circumstance of sexuality which will eventually express itself in our sexual tastes. The time and manner of this decision is the result of decisions taken at an endless number of points in our learning process. Fundamental in these decisions is the relationship between the individual and those who support and supply him/her with protection and needs. Perhaps the most basic troublemaker is that movement within the being that later will express itself as loyalty. Sex is not a problem. What must be examined is what we think about sex.

Can sex be regarded as entertainment or is it strictly for reproduction? The mind always feels that by breaking things up into little pieces and examining them, it will come to understand the whole. The difficulty with this approach is that it is the mind that does the dividing in the first place, and it does this under the illusion that all the divisions are part of the whole. It seems incapable of understanding that no amount of analysis of parts can ever explain the whole, that indeed parts have nothing whatsoever to do with a whole. When the mind sets itself up as the monitor of the body's actions, the result can be nothing but trouble.

It is rare that humans deliberately set out to make a baby. They are generally attracted to

each other for a myriad of reasons, some profound, some superficial, often under the illusion that sex has something to do with love. This attraction seems to have little to do with the actual sex of those attracted to each other. It is an absurd point of view to regard homosexuality as unnatural, for anyone who has lived on a farm has witnessed sexual acts between animals of the same sex. Monkeys of many types practice a submission ritual in which younger males submit to the advances of older males. Can animals commit an unnatural act?

The thoughts that one has about sex are generally socially conditioned, that is, they are the result of cultural organization and nothing more.

A long-time friend of the writer was born a pretty Maharaja in a village in the north of India. He has entertained his friends and his nation (for he is a fine poet in the Punjabi language) for hours, with tales of the sexual intrigues that go on in his village. In northern

India women never look a man in the face, and they will always draw a veil over their eyes when one passes or talks to them. The division between the sexes is very great, yet the most incredible lesions are brought about and sexual promiscuity is rampant. A woman will always call her husband Mister So and So. She will refer to the husband as the daughter's father, never mentioning his name, yet within all of this formality, a look or a casual phrase will speak volumes of affection between two lovers.

In the industrialized society, it has always been the custom to touch male children as little as possible, and to discourage them also from touching others. All intimacy is ritualized. A good example of this is the way businessmen call each other by their first names while making a business deal. Because of the cultural restriction upon touching each other and the restrictions placed upon intimacy in friendships, we get an unbalanced approach to sex which somehow is expected to fulfill many functions other than just sex. The sex act has become the catch-all wherein we expect to realize our completeness. That is not its function and never has been its function, so with these expectations the act will always seem incomplete and eventually a disappointment.

Homosexuality is not just the result of one cause but of many, ranging all the way from habit to revolt against established customs. That there is a connection between homosexuality and submission, there can be no doubt at all. All military groups throughout all ages in all societies have had homosexual cults. Sometimes, as in the American Marines, it is hidden. At other times, as among the Greek or Maya military orders, it has been right out front. Principally it seems that the homosexual response is nature's way of dealing with overcrowding of some form or another. It is one of nature's way of putting a check on population growth.

All of the industrial societies today are caught in the struggle of redefining the role of woman in the society. Since the industrial society is a male-oriented society, this redefinition will not come easily. Yet it is essential and paramount that the 'macho' hold be broken, for men also

must totally redefine their relationship with each other and with their society. The tyranny of one sex over another is unfulfilling and destructive to the individual.

A lot has been said here about homosexuality, but the writer feels this should be looked at closely and the question then asked: Is masturbation sex? On closer examination it is seen that not only homosexuals but heterosexuals as well engage in masturbation, that most of the sexual stimulation comes from the mind and not the body. In masturbation it can be seen that the mind uses the sex organs for its gratification. It is the mind that engages in 'perversion.' It is the mind that forms an attraction for a particular boy or girl and all of that superficial Freudian nonsense is the result of the mind thinking of itself as separate from the body.

One may be surprised to find that we have arrived at a definition of pornography! Let's back up a little. The mind has been trained by the culture (motion pictures and the like) to find all those who look like Rock Hudson, for example, as sexually attractive, so that if you

do not look like Mr. Hudson or Tony Curtis, or Betty Grable, you are considered not sexually attractive. The mind knows the body does not look like any of the above persons so the mind becomes dissatisfied with the body and dislike of the self develops. Because one dislikes one's own body there is no reason to feel others will be attracted to one, so that when others are attracted the first reaction is suspicion. There cannot be any satisfaction out of any relationship based upon self-hatred, so more and more the mind exploits the body, more and more the fantasy needed to excite the mind becomes extreme. Eventually fantasy takes over, and sexual behavior becomes more bizarre. Sadism, masochism, humiliation, transvestitism, all of these are engaged in as confusion mounts within the mind in its search for satisfaction. The mind uses cosmetics and make-up to make the body less like itself and perhaps more like Betty Grable, or Queen Victoria, or whoever is the idol of the time.

Pornography is the product of self-hatred.

Sex is part of life, no more important or less important than a star or a flower. It can only provide satisfaction when it is not overloaded with expectations. Sex, like food, can supply satisfaction for a vast variety of reasons. (Simple hunger makes things taste good, but a good cook is the one who by orchestrating all of the components raises eating to the status of an art.)

Sex has never been just for reproduction. It has been the one action that has shown people the need and dependence they inevitably have for and on each other. The message here is no different than all of the others: harmony within oneself creates harmony in the world around one.

This beautiful piece of caligraphy is taken from the Dresden Codex. It is a section dealing with the phases of the moon. The stories that the ordinary people tell of the moon's doings, say that it was she who discovered sex, and became a complete wanton (fickle, inconstant, moon, in almost every culture). There is one bizarre drawing of her refusing to have sex with the god of death, although there is another equally bizarre in which she is caught in the act with the Death God. She had many lovers, for her children are the stars. Her husband was the Sun, and his anger over her behavior is said to be what causes the eclipses. Needless to say the priests view of the whole matter was very different.

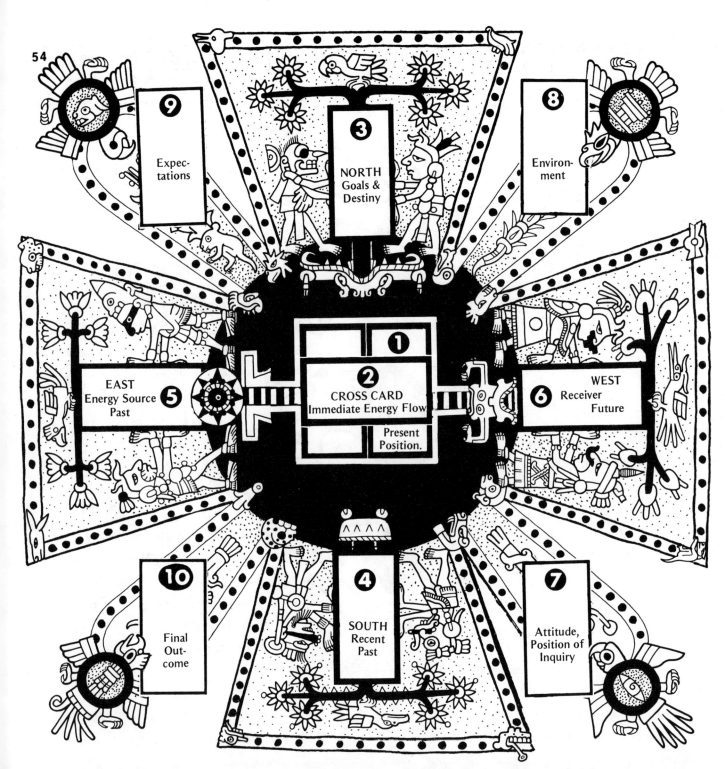

Unlocking

USING THE SPREAD

Select any card which may best suit the Question (if any). Place it face up in the center of the table. SHUFFLE the remainder of the deck while concentrating on the question. TURN UP the cards in the following order.

1 TURN UP first card and place it next to the key card. This is called the cover card and it represents the present position of the questioner in relation to the key card.

2 TURN UP the second card and place it across the two previous cards. This is called the cross card, and it reveals the immediate influence of the energy flowing in the situation.

3 TURN UP the third card and place it above the other cards. It is the North card and will reveal the goals and destiny of the matter in question.

4 TURN UP the fourth card, place it below the central group of cards. It is the South card and it will reveal the recent past events. The foundation, or the reason for the question.

5 TURN UP the fifth card, place it to the left of the central group. It is the East card and represents the energy source and how it moves towards future events.

6 TURN UP the sixth card, place it to the right of the key. This is the West card, it represents the recipient of the energy flowing in the situation. Both card 5 and 6 may face towards the key, or turn away from the key in several different combinations. If the East card is reversed it shows the difficulties or obstructions in the past. If the West card is reversed, the difficulties lie in the Future.

7 TURN UP the seventh card, place it to the right of the south card at the bottom of the spread. This card shows the key's attitude or position in the circumstance.

8 TURN UP the eighth card, place it to the right of the north card on the top. It shows the environment and tendencies at work in the case.

9 TURN UP the ninth card, and place it to the left of the north card. It will show the inner emotions, the hopes and fears in the matter.

10 TURN UP the tenth card and place it to the left of the South card. It will show the final results in the matter. If it is a Court Card, it will represent a person involved in the question asked, and a new reading should be done using that card as the key, so that the person's attitude may be revealed. If the result is vague or of a dubious nature, use that last card as the key and repeat the process until there is understanding.

The Four Corners Of The Self

ALLED "THE CROSS OF QUETZALCOATL" TO DIVINE THE NATURE OF POSSIBILITIES

THE METHOD OF SHUFFLING THE CARDS

Take the cards out of the box and place them face down in front of you on a table that has been previously cleared for use. Relax. Close the eyes and let the cares and preoccupations of the day slip away. You have plenty of time.

You will have noticed that the cards are considerably larger than ordinary playing cards. Most tarot cards are large, and shuffling them in the ordinary manner is rather difficult, although not impossible. The standard method of shuffling in the hand is not used for tarot cards, however, as the purpose of the shuffle is not only to mix the cards but also to get some of them upside down. This is accomplished by dividing the deck into two packets of about the same size and putting them in front of you. Next place the palms of the hands upon the top cards of the packets and commence to turn the cards in a circular manner, mixing both packets together, as you see in the diagram below:

Keep this up until all of the cards are thoroughly mixed. Take your time and use the motion to clear the mind. You may use the hands in any way you wish, but the motion must always be in the same direction. Do not reverse the motion of mixing because you will begin to turn those reversed cards back to their original position. It will require a little practice, but it is soon mastered. There are several other methods of shuffling, any one of which may be used. This one is selected as being the simplest and the one that helps induce the right mood in the user of the cards.

CHOOSING THE KEY CARD

You may have already decided which card you will use to represent the person for whom you plan to do the reading, or to represent the question or situation that you wish to investigate. If not, this is the time to make the selection. There are also many methods of doing this. It is advised that except for the next cut of the cards, the owner of the cards never let another person handle the deck. Place the key card in position on the table where you will lay the spread. Now make one packet of the cards and place them face down in front of the other person. Ask the person to make one cut of the cards, usually with the left (non-dominant) hand (if this is a reading for you, you do this movement). This is done three times, then you gather the cards back into one packet and begin the spread.

If the Key is to represent a man, select one of the Lord cards. You will find the various qualities of each listed in the index. A woman would of course be represented by a Lady card. A young person of either sex would be represented by a Servant card; a husband, wife, or lover by one of the Warrior cards. It may also be good to use the higher arcana card that represents the zodiacal sign of the person, if that is known and thought to be applicable. A journey as a Key could be the six of Swords. There are no absolute rules as to how to proceed, however, and it is up to each person to work their vision with the cards and not to be blindly bound by rules. The Key may simply be a card that appeals to the reader upon a casual glance. There are readers who do not use a Key at all but simply allow the reading to unfold, for they feel that the Key is implicit within the reading and better left unstated.

METHOD OF LAYING OUT A SPREAD

The cards are to be removed from the one packet which you have placed in front of you, leaving room around, below, and above the Key, placing the spread easily and uncramped by the following method. Pick up the top card between the thumb and index finger of whichever hand you feel at ease (preferably the

left or non-dominant hand) and place the card face up on the table in a movement that is away from you. You will notice that this has the effect of reversing the card from the way it lies in the packet. See the diagram that follows.

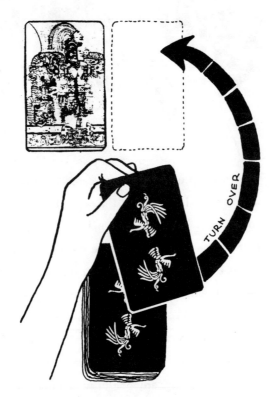

You may also remove the cards from the side, or towards you. Practice all movements and study what happens. The above method is

recommended, but whatever method you choose, that is the one you must use throughout the spread. YOU MUST NOT CHANGE in the middle of the spread. Make a habit of always using the same method when laying the spread.

THE CROSS OF QUETZALCOATL

Study the design of the cross at the beginning of this chapter. It may look rather complicated but it isn't really so difficult. The one thing you may notice is that cards are marked North, South, East and West, and that the East seems to be on the wrong side. It isn't wrong, for this is the night sky, as used in astrology. If you place the design overhead and look up at it as if at the sky, with the East in the right direction, you will see that all of the other points now line up in their proper directions.

Now let's begin the spread. You have the key in place on the table. Next to it, on your right, place the first card and across these two place card number two. (A very practiced reader can many times get a whole reading from these three cards alone.) Next place card number three in the north (above), number four in the south (below), number five to the east (left), and number six to the West (right). This is the first part of the cross and we will examine it before proceeding further.

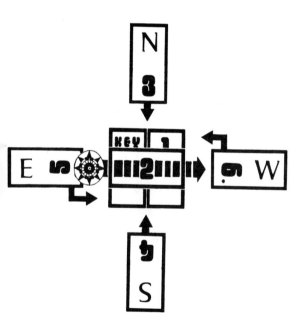

To be right way up, all cards must face in towards the center, so that the south card appears upside down to the reader when it is the right way up. The arrows in the diagram above indicate the correct way a card is to face so that it is not inverted. Next notice the

East card, then card number two, then the card in the West. This set indicates the movement of energy in the situation under investigation. The sun rises in the east and appears to move toward the west. This is a movement of rising energy, of rising force. That movement would be unobstructed if card 5 faced the center, card 2 faced card 6, and card 6 faced the center. If card 2 faced card 5, the energy would be in decline, with life leaving the situation under observation. 5 and 6 may both be reversed, a sign that the energy is absent, or the cards may be all mixed, obviously an indicator of uncertain energy in the situation. Examine the possibilities that manifest themselves in these three cards, for they are crucial to an understanding of the energies involved.

Now look at the picture on card number 1. How is it placed? Always note first if the card is inverted or not. This card shows the present position (relationship) of the inquiry to the Key. Card number 2 shows the direction of energy and the immediate influence upon the Key card. Card 5 is the past influence; card 6 is the influence of the future upon the Key. Card 3, the North card, shows aims (goals) and

ideals. Card 4, the south card, shows the foundation, the basis of the inquiry.

Now place the next four cards in the four corners, cards 7, 8, 9, 10, just as in the diagram below.

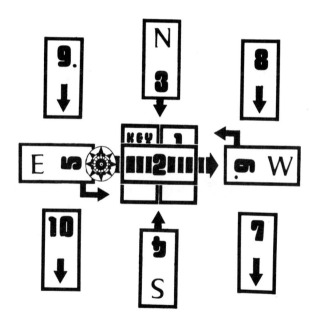

Card 7 relates directly to the inquirer as expressed through the Key card. Look carefully at it, remembering and integrating all that has gone before. Card 8 is placed top right and will show you the environment of the Key. Card 9, placed top left, will tell you what the expectations are in the matter under examination. Card 10, at left bottom, will give the final outcome.

Examine the final outcome card. It may not be clear, or it may represent a person. A person usually is one of the "court" cards, and might represent the doctor in a medical question, or the judge in a legal one (if that is the case, another reading should be done using the "court" card as the Key). This way the attitude of the key person may be established. Depending on the complexity of the question, it may be seen that several readings would likely be the rule rather than the exception.

However, let the cards decide that. Remember there are no demands made upon you. Let the information flow and what is to be done will become clear. The reading of the tarot is not something that happens overnight. It takes practice to set up the right mood and allow information to flow in an uninterrupted manner. The whole purpose is to "short circuit" the thinking brain and allow the intuitive faculties to take over. It is a process much like changing bands on an AM/FM radio. If you wish to listen to the FM stations you must shut off the AM. Mentally, few people can do this immediately. Indeed it cannot be done, it must be allowed to happen. Any attempt at control will only impede the whole process of switching over. There is nothing to fear, for all that one allows to happen is that the so-called rational mind (left brain)—that is, learned systems of logic—is switched off and a contact with less readily explained phenomena is permitted. These processes are no less real, except that any attempt at rational explanation does not serve to clarify them. In other words, you will begin to see possibilities which would not 'normally' occur to you.

FORTELLING THE FUTURE

The writer does not think it is possible to foretell the future with any accuracy, except by people with special talent, but understands that it is very possible to pick up on certain predictable possibilities. Here is a good opportunity to examine time, which like all simple things requires what may seem to be a complex explanation. Time and its passage is but movement and memory. What that means is that if any one of these qualities is missing, time cannot exist. A lifetime is just that, for a person or a gnat, regardless of how it is measured. I am forty-three years old, that is, since we measure time by the passage of the earth round the sun, forty-three of these have occurred since I was born. Or if we registered a year by the moon, I would be about five hundred and sixteen moon years old. Now if we look we can see that time exists in the head, not in the external world. Something happened, not during this moon but two moons ago. I remember the moons. If I did not, time would not be. Without memory, time is not. Yet I age. This is just a cultural way of seeing the accumulation of effects in the body. If time does not exist except in the mind, then also the view of life passed, stored in the mind and called the past, is not the real past at all but a remembered view of what occurred. There is no past, and therefore there cannot be such a thing as history, except as the writer's viewpoint of what is believed to have occurred. With no history there cannot be any future either.

Perhaps it would be clearer if we look at an

example, the sinking of the unsinkable ship, the Titanic. The ship did sink. There were predictions that the ship would sink, and at least two people refused to sail on her because they believed she would sink. None of this is deniable, all is proven, in that it is recorded as having happened. Now if no one knew about it, could it be said to have happened? No. Then it could not be said except generally, such as, "ships do sink, and no one knows about them!" We have disposed of that question and are still left with a ship called the Titanic that at this moment presumably lies at the bottom of the ocean somewhere. It is a very good example, for it is a YES/NO situation. She was loudly touted as unsinkable, but some people felt the decided possibility that the Titanic would sink, an either/or situation. The odds against the sinking must have been very great. But with every ship, no matter how unsinkable, there always remains the possibility of a disaster.

Every nuclear plant, no matter how safe, has a very dangerous possibility. Every airplane that flies has the possibility of crashing. So disaster is always possible to predict, because it is inherent.

Now to say the Titanic will sink on April 15th, 1912, at 7:30 p.m. is a different matter. To say it two weeks in advance is also a very strange thing. We see that time is a cultural event and that it has a psychological being as well. So how could these two unrelated phenomena, an event and the time of the event, be brought together? In this inquiry it seems that it is possible to bring a real event and a made event together on what may be more than a hit or miss basis. How this coming together occurs is a mystery. That it is outside the rational system, that it does not compute, that it is not logical there is no doubt. Yet it does occur and can be sensed. It just cannot be examined or explained. It seems to indicate that there is a place within the brain/mind where non-rational experiences have a logical but non-connected expression, a way of being that can only express itself when the intellectualizing, order-making, connecting mechanism is switched off. We are not talking about madness, just that sort of experiencing that cannot be talked about, because it cannot be expressed in words. There is a fantastic amount of concepts which have no verbal form in the English language because they have not been thought of or are of little interest. The English of five hundred years ago did not have any words at all dealing with the operation of the mind, because it was not of any interest to those who used the language. When it became of interest, Greek words were used because they already existed. The Greeks thought about such things and so had words for them. The Eskimo people have no word for war. Portuguese defines four different categories of sexy. Only within the writer's lifetime has the word sexy entered the everyday language of English, because we now define what non-sexy is and we do this by giving a value to its opposite, sexy. The tarot is an excellent tool to develop a familiarity with experiencing that which cannot be communicated—not a denial of communication but a direct, unselfconscious contact, a tool to discover that this contact is real yet not talked about, a tool to directly examine the operating of the unknown.

THE READING OF THE TAROT SPREAD

There must first of all be a distance, a lack of personal involvement between the reader and the spread. Do you remember how in the game

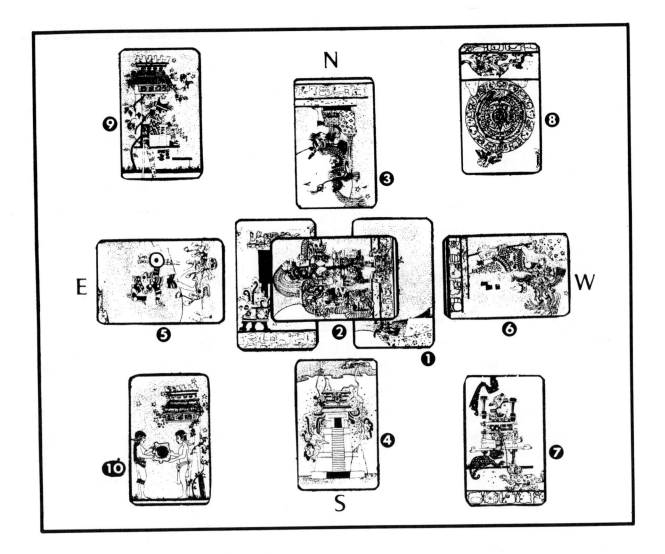

whether he will express ideas well or if the reader will understand what he is trying to do. Since it relates to this work it will be possible for the reader in the future to see how well the reading stands up, for it will relate to an actual event, the publishing and continuance of the Maya Tarot Codex.

QUESTION: Will the author achieve the goal he has set in writing this work?

The first thing to notice about the spread is that it has only three inverted cards, the Consort in the North, the Tower in the South, and the Wheel in the eighth position. That is a small number of inverted cards and it indicates that it is an upward mobile spread. Next note the energy, also excellent, moving positively from East to West. So all indications are that this is a very upward moving layout. Now let's look at each card individually.

KEY: Selected because the question deals with wisdom and the aims of that wisdom, the Sage (●●●●) seems to be a good card to use.

CARD 1: The Fool (⬭). A good card expressing clearly the present position of the inquirer.

of solitaire (evolved from tarot meditations), there is an awareness that expresses itself as a prohibition of cheating. This is what is meant by distance, the ability to stand aside from the self and see how the outcome will express itself, to observe the working of fate, without involvement.

Observe the spread pictured above. Look at it carefully and note the placement of the cards. This is an actual spread, using only the cards of the higher arcana. The writer threw this spread after having selected the Sage card (●●●●) as the Key. That card was selected because this is the writer's first book, and he has doubts about

He is dealing with the unknown and has entered a new field, one in which he is unfamiliar and in which there is little guidance available from others. The success of the card depends upon an ability to go with the flow of circumstances.

CARD 2: The Ruler (••••). The immediate influence is the card of creation by will and power. It faces the right direction and is in the place of the energy source, a most powerful card to have in this position. It represents realization in action. A very auspicious card here, nothing vague about it at all. It says the energy is available, use it!

CARD 3: The Consort (•••) inverted. Since this is the position of destiny, it seems a distinct warning to watch the self with great care. In this position the Consort can sap the vitality of the Ruler card; but because of the strength of the Ruler, it would be safe to interpret the Consort as a warning of possible stormy weather ahead on an ego level. This is the card of manipulation and a warning of the difficulties of remaining true to the orginal goals.

CARD 4: The Tower (≜) inverted. Here we

have the basis of the inquiry, the foundation of the questioner's query. Does the inquirer wish to turn the established order on its head? Inverted, this is the card of accident and destruction, but those are not to be interpreted negatively in this spread, for this is the card of liberation, of release. The suggestion here is that the achievement of goals will come by accident. The release necessary to express the unknown will come about in spite of the efforts of the inquirer.

CARD 5: Death (≣). This card is in the East, the place of rising energy, an excellent card to have here as it signifies the end of the old and the beginning of the new. A new day, a new movement. This is the card of the future and it indicates the death of the past.

CARD 6: The Priest (▬). This is the card of the transmitter of knowledge, at home in the past. The Priest is the servant of the society he serves, and is bound to serve it well in this position. This is a very beautiful energy spread, the movement from Death through the Ruler to the Priest, full of almost irrepressible energy that will be of great service to humankind.

CARD 7: The Warrior (••). The card of victory, good news, and openness, revealing the questioner himself. His ideals seem to be of the highest. The card indicates a willingness to move, to inquire in an open and forthright manner, aware that what may be seen as a mistake is really a learning opportunity. This is the card of speech and care in expression. It indicates a concern in framing the question, so that it will reveal and hide at the same time. It also indicates that the goals will be realized through an ability to communicate through speech. Well aspected.

CARD 8: The Wheel (≡) inverted. This is the card of learning, in the position of environment. Inverted it implies repetition and recurrence. Given the present environment, it seems the questioner will of necessity repeat whatever is basic to an understanding of the message. There will be endless repetition (such as a lecture tour). Since this follows on from the Warrior card, the card of speech, it seems that the repetition will be by speech, by demand of the situation that the questioner finds himself in at this time.

CARD 9: The Priestess (••). This is the place of

expectations and the inner emotions. The Priestess is the card of mixed emotions, of divided attention. It is easy to see that it is with no little trepidation that the questioner enters upon the journey towards the set goal. There is also little doubt that the energy will be available to overcome the doubtful nature of this card; if it were reversed then decided difficulties would come about from self indulgence. Fortunately this card smiles on the endeavor and aids it in overcoming the setback of the Consort.

CARD 10: The Lovers (☋). The final outcome is the card of the two halves joined, the card of inspiration and love. It is the card of the gathering together of experience. It displays the known and the unknown working together in love, and without a doubt points to a very successful outcome.

QUESTION: Will the author achieve the goal he has set in writing this work?
SUMMARY OF THE SPREAD: The goal itself has been carefully left unstated. However,

the spread indicates that it has a very powerful push behind it, that it is in the nature of service and will necessitate a great deal of repetition. It seems that the task did not originate in the highest of ideals, but that the circumstances of the situation will carry things through to a conclusion that will alter both the questioner and, most importantly, the perception he has of what he believes he is doing. The work will be a success, but not for the reasons the questioner thinks, and not in the way he thinks.

CARE OF THE CARDS

Since the cards are to mirror the hidden parts of oneself, they must be accorded respect and treated with care and attention. There are those who keep two sets of cards, one for their own use and another for use when doing read-

ings for others. Their own deck is kept wrapped in silk and as much as possible never allowed to be seen or handled by others.

Since silk is a resister of electrical current, it forms a neat barrier against the confusing mixture of external vibrations. It also acts as a Generator of Electrical current and so acts like a Faraday Cage. It isolates the vibrations built up within the cards from external contact.

RESPECT IS THE KEY WORD, the cards should not be treated as a party amusement toy. They are a very serious tool for the examination of the self.

CEREMONIAL MAGIC AND THE CARDS

For those interested in this aspect, there are many ceremonies attached to the use of the cards. They do serve the purpose of isolating one from the mundane events of the day and prepare the mind for the work ahead. The writer favors a simple approach, for ceremony can become so complex that it overshadows the very reason that it is used.

Many writers cannot think until they sit at their typewriter, or can only think as they write in long hand. Ceremony serves the same purpose. The writer suggests the use of a simple vestment, like a priest's stole. Perhaps it can be beautifully embroidered. It can also function as a wrap for the cards so that they are kept both together. A suggested design is presented for those who feel a need for this approach.

This design has the advantage of being simple and suitable for both sexes to wear.

It should be made only in 100% natural materials and lined with silk. The colors should be bright and clear. It can be decorated with embroidery in beautiful patterns. It can be fringed and beaded. If the Feathered Serpent design is used, that is fine, provided it is for your own use, and not a commercial endeavor.

The design of the stole can be varied to suit one's own taste, though it should be kept relatively simple so that it folds over the pocket and makes a neat package.

POCKET

FLAP | BACK | FRONT

8"

←3"→ | ←5½"→ | ←5½"→

HALF STOLE w/POCKET.

← 18" →

← STITCH TWO ⅛ together →

← 36" →

The Great Cross, Spread:  BEING AN ENLAR

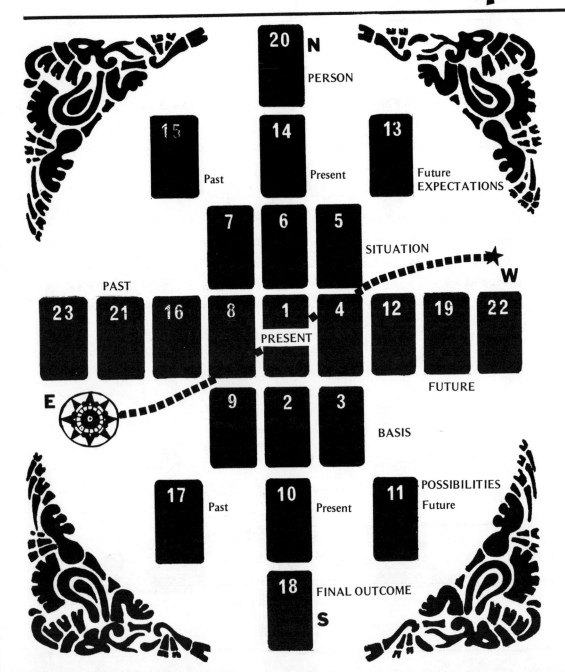

This is a larger spread that is used to gain more detailed information. It is prepared in a different way than the Quetzalcoatl Cross spread. No Key card is used at all; instead twenty-three cards are picked at random from the shuffled deck. The deck is then put aside and the twenty-three cards shuffled again, then separated into three packets with the left hand (right hand for those who are left-handed). The reader places the three packets together and proceeds in the usual manner to lay out the spread.

The spread is laid out in a spiral, beginning in the center with card number one, until all of the cards are turned up and make the design pictured here. Card number 20 represents the person for whom the reading is being done (it can represent the reader as well). Cards 15, 14, and 13 represent the EXPECTATIONS of the person (20). All of the situations in the spread have three cards, except the person (20) and the outcome (18). Where there are three cards they always are the past, present and future of the expectations (except when dealing with the past or future, then it is the near, middle and far past or far future).

Cards 7, 6, and 5 represent the SITUATION about which the inquirer harbors expectations. The FUTURE is represented by cards 12, 19, and 22, the PRESENT by cards 8, 1, and 4, and the PAST by cards 23, 21, and 16. The BASIS, the reason for the inquiry, is represented by cards 9, 2, and 3. The POSSIBILITIES inherent within the inquiry are represented in cards number 17, 10, and 11. The FINAL OUTCOME is represented by card number 18.

Because this is such a large spread and deals with much more information, it requires a great deal more practice to weld the information contained within it into a cogent pattern.

Just as in the smaller spread the first thing to look for is the energy within the spread. Is it rising or is it on the decline? Next observe the number of reversed cards in the spread. As a general rule this will tell you if the situation is a negative or a positive one. Care must be exercised in observation of the reversed cards, for if any of the higher arcana cards numbered

4 (⋯), 9 (⋮⋮), 14 (☰), or 19 (☰) are present and are reversed, they may be turned the right way up as they are not diminished by being reversed.

Having observed the energy state in the situation and seen whether the situation is inclined more towards a negative or a positive and balanced condition, you will have a general measure that will help you in the observation of each card in its position.

Begin with card number 20 at the top of the spread. This card functions as a Key card and will tell you about the person for whom the reading is being done. In like manner all of the cards are read in groups of three, starting at the top and ending at the bottom with card number 18. It is the final outcome and should be a crisp and clear situation. If it is vague and does not seem to apply, it may be due to the energy in the spread. A good detailed reading from this spread can easily take an hour and a half, so don't hurry it. Always be relaxed and do not force anything. If part of the reading is not clear to you, go on to the next section. As

the situation becomes clearer, return to the part that wasn't clear. When you gather experience you will be able to jump about the spread and examine different parts of it, becoming aware of its general content. You must always return to the top, however, and read downward in a final summation.

Remember that in the end you are the final arbiter. If you are not happy with what has occurred in the spread, do it again. You will eventually discover your own way of going about a reading and this is encouraged by the writer. THERE IS NO CORRECT WAY OF DOING A SPREAD. It is up to you. Some people are faster than others, but this is not important. The writer knows a reader who is very slow and manifests little confidence, yet is able to give a very accurate reading. After all, the accuracy of the reading is the most important part. Do not feel that there is a right and a wrong way of reading the cards. The information comes from you, not the cards. They are, after all, only the mirror in which the seeing takes place.

• The

The four triangles at the center of the Mandala represent the warrior cards

 Fire The Warrior of STAFFS.
Air. The Warrior of SWORDS.
Water. The Warrior of CUPS.
Earth. The Warrior of JADES.

The astrological houses that serve the cards of the higher arcana on the outermost circle (white) are named and the letter next to each house are

C. CARDINAL SIGNS: Aries, Cancer, Libra, Capricorn.

F. FIXED SIGNS: Taurus, Leo, Scorpio, Aquarius.

M. MUTABLE SIGNS: Gemini, Virgo, Sagittarius, Pisces.

The planetary signs are drawn in the following manner:

	SUN.
	MOON.
	MERCURY.
	VENUS.
	MARS.
	JUPITER.
	SATURN.
	URANUS.
	NEPTUNE.
	PLUTO.

At the time that the writer was painting the Xultun Tarot deck, he was informed that there was astrological information that could be applied to each card. The writer has only a very rudimentary knowledge of astrology. He was supplied with the signs and put them on the cards. When it came time to prepare this book, he was at a loss to make sense of that aspect and read half a dozen books, each one saying something different. Then he approached a friend, Glen Dixon, who has a reputation as an astrologer who inquires into things with a keen eye. Glen agreed to examine the signs on the cards and discover the order therein.

The result was this beautiful mandala and an order far surpassing anything that the writer had previously tried. A little study will make clear just how the cards relate to astrology.

Since astrology is a discipline, with its own study and relationships, it would require a whole book to explore that subject alone, which is not possible within the scope of this account of the cards. Glen, however, has been so kind as to write an essay demonstrating to those who already have a knowledge of astrology, the tarot layout, and how it works. The writer wishes to take this opportunity to thank Glen for his help so openly and unstintingly given.

Common Roots of Astrology and the Xultun Tarot

by

Glen Wayne Dixon

The usefulness of an organized set of psychological symbols lies in its ability to represent and reflect corresponding meanings which exist within the psyche, far below the threshold of consciousness. These meanings do not allow for a more direct means of access, for we cannot turn our eyes upon ourselves—we must use a looking-glass for that purpose. The person who actively practices a discipline based upon such a set of symbols is a person who learns to freely project himself upon the archetypal images and perceive the workings of his own psyche in them. The process of learning such a discipline is the process of building these synchronistic connections between the subjective and objective realms, between meaning and symbol. Gradually, through this process of projection, one can learn how he gives meaning to and is reflected in all things, can learn that what he previously experienced as being "out there" is really "in here." Slowly, the disowned parts of the self are re-absorbed, the split between the inner and outer man is healed. The person is made whole, reunited with the universe and with the flow of life. It is not surprising that C. G. Jung practiced both Astrology and the I Ching, for he fully understood how symbols could mirror psychic events within the person, and how they could be used to greatly further self-knowledge and integration.

This is a book about the Xultun Tarot, and to the student of these enigmatic images (such as myself) who first learned to make the connection with a different set of symbols, it is helpful to relate one to the other and thus utilize the psychological groundwork that took so much time and energy to construct. This chapter is for persons with some familiarity with the symbols of Astrology (which should include most everyone) who would like to use this basis to better approach and understand the Tarot. I offer my experience in relating the two not as a substitute for the reader seeing his own uniquely personal meanings in the cards, but rather (hopefully) as a catalyst to spark off these associations.

There are various methods of correlating the symbols of Astrology and the Tarot, all of which are awkward to some extent due to the different numerological divisions of the respective systems. These differences become more pronounced as one proceeds farther into fine detail. Astrology, for example, places a great deal of emphasis on the number twelve, probably because there are twelve new moons or conjunctions of the Sun and Moon in a year. This number is unimportant in the Tarot, which instead emphasizes the number ten, a number that was of little use in Astrology until the discovery of Pluto in 1930 increased to ten the number of major celestial bodies in use (the

Sun, Moon, and 8 other planets). The division of the Major Arcana into 22 lends itself more to comparisons with the Kabbalistic Tree of Life than with Astrology. At the root of both Astrology and the Tarot, however, is the division of the whole by the number four, and it is in comparisons at this basic numerological level that we can find a common meeting ground for the two unique conceptual systems. It is likewise in the basic experiences that consitute the foundations of human life that we can find meanings which they share. For these reasons I will direct my comments to comparisons at this common level rather than attempt detailed and exhaustive interpretations of each individual card, which could not be explained in astrolgoical terms alone and at any rate will be done elsewhere in this book.

It should also be noted that the astrological symbols found on the cards or assigned to them are but parts of the larger symbols, rather than being wholly representative of or synonymous with them.

We use a complex organization of symbols rather than a single one in order to fully reflect the multi-faceted nature of life, and while it is important to remember that the various

symbols in a set represent different aspects of a unitary whole, it is also necessary to make sharp distinctions between them. This makes possible specificity and detail. As soon as you define something, say what it is, you also say what it *isn't*. If a symbol means anything and everything, then it means nothing. For this reason, organizing a coherent set of symbols begins with a process of division. This is the process by which the facets of life are differentiated, categorized, and assigned to the various cards of the deck as well as to the planets, signs, houses, aspects, etc. This conscious analytical process is valid only if it reflects a deeper natural organization, however, rather than being purely contrived and superficial. This is the only way we can forge the link between the conscious and unconscious worlds.

In Astrology, the unit of the year (one cycle of the Earth around the Sun) is first divided into four seasons. From one point of view this is an arbitrary distinction, since one season flows into the next and nowhere is a clear division experienced. Yet these divisions, while imaginary in the sense that the earth's equator is imaginary, are likewise based upon undeniable matematical realities, in this case the relationship between the axis of the Earth and the plane of the Solar System. This relationship gives rise to the four cardinal points of the Earth's orbit—the solstices and equinoxes. A line from solstice to solstice halves the year, another from equinox to equinox quarters it. These four seasons are further subdivided into periods of three months (or moons) each. This interaction between the numbers three and four produces the twelve signs of the Zodiac, which are simply phases of the cycle of the seasons to which they are tied inseparably, deriving their meanings from this natural cyclic progression. Seen from the Earth, the Sun enters the sign of Aries on the first day of Spring each year, because the Vernal Equinox is by definition the cusp (or beginning) of Aries.

The division of the four seasons is reflected in the Tarot in the division of the Lower Arcana into four suits, and most specifically in the numbered cards of these suits. The Swords correlate to the season of Spring, the Staffs to Summer, Cups to Autumn, and Jades to Winter. Thus the first three Swords wear the symbol for Aries, the first of the Spring signs, the second three wear Taurus, which follows, and the third triplet wear Gemini, the last of the Spring signs. The signs are further subdivided into three *decanates* each (called so because each represents a span of ten days: 30 - 3 = 10); each card representing one decanate of the appropriate sign and adorned with the symbol for the planetary sub-ruler of that decanate along with that of its sign. Thus the Ace of Swords is correlated to the Mars decanate, or first third, of Aries, the Two to the Sun decanate, and so on. The idea here is to show the change and progression that takes place within a sign as well as from sign to sign. The Aces of each suit are especially important in understanding the root idea of that suit, for they correlate to the cardinal points themselves. For this reason we will pay special attention to them. Since ten is the number of completion, the Tens can be thought of as representing the culmination of that season as a whole and therefore wear no individual symbols.

Given these correlations, what meanings are suggested? Rather than idly speculating, let us consider the nature of the seasons themselves. We can see that the half of the year from the beginning of Spring to the end of Summer (when the days are longer than the nights) is a time of the expression of light and energy, when life flourishes and pushes outwards, whereas in the Fall and Winter we witness the retreat of life, a withdrawal and a resting and storing of energy. Therefore we can say that Swords and Staffs represent the extroverted, expansive, assertive facets of life, while Cups and Jades show the introverted, collecting, and preserving phases. We can also hypothesize that since the length of days increases through Winter and Spring and decreases through Summer and Autumn, the Sun being the symbol of the radiant center or the Self, we can say that Jades and Swords represent self-increase, or personal matters, whereas Staffs and Cups symbolize self-decrease, or non-personal matters. Combining the two, we can say that Swords signify the assertion of the personal, the world of individuality and competition; Staffs signify the assertion of the non-personal, the world of creativity and unselfish action; Cups represent the preserving of the non-personal, the world of maintaining relationships and security; and Jades represent the preserving of the personal, the world of resources and business.

Becoming more specific, Spring is a time of great energy and growth, but also of great effort and strain. The new life striving to exist is still young and undeveloped and has many obstacles to overcome, although possessed of the superabundant vigor of youth with which to accomplish this task. Therefore Swords are cards of initiative, enterprise, courage, struggle, difficulty, strife, victory and defeat, life and death. The Ace pictures a sword rising out of the ground like a new plant. It has pierced its way into the light and stands ready to fight for its place in the sun, having already dealt a blow on this account. This is the card of the Mars decanate of Aries—Mars, god of war, whose symbol resembles the sword and shield or the erect penis; Aries, whose symbol is the battering ram charging with lowered head—appropriate ornaments for the first card of the suit representing the will to live, audacity and forcefulness, the will to be free and willingness to struggle against any and all who try to limit or repress this freedom.

Summer is the season of completion, when flowering and growth are achieved. Multiplication has led to a state of abundance, difficulty gives way to ease and the rewards of past efforts are reaped. Staffs are cards of activity, successful enterprise, energetic expression, enthusiasm, joy, recreation, strength and mastery. The Ace shows a bowl overflowing with the fires of life, a symbol of vitality and creative potency. The symbols indicating the Moon decanate of Cancer may at first seem inappropriate, for what could these watery symbols of the mother, home, instinct, devotion, receptivity, and dependency have to do with the fiery brilliance of Summer? It reminds us that life was born in the sea, that creation takes place in the womb (symbolized by the bowl containing the flames) where the creative spark is nurtured and brought forth. The flame pictured on the card, while radiantly outgoing and positive, is also yielding and dependent. It is forever bound and rooted to its fuel, its source. Likewise it is in the Summer, when life is at its height, that we are the most lazy and passive. We lounge around the pool and absorb the life-giving rays. The root power of Staffs is revealed here, for to manifest great creative force is to become totally receptive and open to it, to provide a receptacle and fuel for it, to surrender completely to it and let it work spontaneously and intuitively through one. It is the ego which is offered up as fuel for the creative fire.

With Autumn we reach a stage of equilibrium. The nights begin to be longer than the days. Life begins to withdraw into the seed, retreating from the extensions. The bounty of the harvest is taken indoors and stored to equalize the deficiencies of the season. Cups are cards dealing with intake, the satisfaction of needs and deficiencies, of decreasing what is too much so that what is too little can be increased, of making whole and complete. For this reason they have much to do with human relationships, especially partnerships, through which we seek to make up for what we lack. Selfishness and independence must be sacrificed so that relationships may grow. The Ace shows a large cup, a symbol of containment, of keeping inside. An empty cup yearns to be filled. It is also adorned with flowers, symbols of art, fragrance, sweetness, romance, attraction, and sex, and with a bird, symbol of music and levity. The correlation is to the Venus decanate of Libra, symbols of balance, harmony, affection, cooperation, and peace. Autumn is the most beautiful time of the year, when the foliage turns riotous with color and the days are mellow and gentle. This beauty is the result of the inward turning of life, just as beauty is magnetic—it pulls inwards rather than pushes outwards. The symbol for Venus, which resembles a hand-held mirror, shows that this inward turning can take the form of narcissism and vanity, or of the soul-searching and self-knowledge that comes from working out our relationships and seeing ourselves reflected in others.

In Winter the withdrawal of life becomes complete. The vegetation has died and life lies dormant in the seed, waiting to be awakened by the warmth of Spring. Many animals retreat into safety and seclusion to rest and conserve energy. Long nights and cold weather encourage indoor activities and longer periods of sleep. This is not a state of permanent repose, however, but a quiet preparation for future enterprises. It can be a most productive season, just as the cold incites some creatures to migrate and can make us feel more awake and motivate us to be more physically active. Jades are cards of patient industry, self-defense, accumulation of resources, practical necessity, "getting it together," worldly and mundane affairs of all kinds. The Ace is adorned with symbols of growth and protection and is correlated to the Saturn decanate of Capricorn, symbolic of paternity, authority, limitation, ambition, responsibility and discipline. It is the severity of Winter which teaches us the value of caution, prudence, and preparation. It is times of limitation that teach us to come down to earth (like the snake on the card) and manifest our potentials in concrete form. It also illustrates the danger that we may des-

cend to the lowest level, succumb to greed and possessiveness, harden into cynical selfishness and egotism. Through the impersonal feedback of reality we learn that we get from life what we put into it and therefore must accept the responsibility for our actions, and that the rewards of honest effort are well worth the price of paying our dues.

Thus we do arrive back at Spring and complete the cycle, reminding us that the Tarot (Taro= Rota, a wheel) is a cyclic and self-renewing whole rather than a linear progression with a beginning and an end.

The twelvefold division of the year into four seasons of three months each is not the only way that the numbers three and four interact to provide a general ordering and classification of the Zodiac (and by attribution the Tarot). Even more prevalent and useful is the classification of the twelve signs into four *elements* of three *modes* (or *qualities*) each. These elements are Fire, Earth, Air, and Water, and the modes are known as Cardinal, Fixed, and Mutable. The elements are located alternately around the wheel, beginning with Fire and proceeding in the order given, so that the signs of each element form an equilateral triangle rather

than a group as in the case of the seasons. The modes are likewise alternately assigned and it will be noted that the Cardinal signs are those of the solstices and equinoxes. In this way the signs begin to take on individuality, for while there are three each of the Fire, Earth, Air, and Water signs and four each of the Cardinal, Fixed, and Mutable signs, there is only one Cardinal Fire, one Fixed Earth, and so on.

The concept of the four elements reflects the tendency in nature to separate and stratify into a hierarchy of levels and densities, an idea implicit in the symbolism of the images themselves. This concept is applicable to many different areas of life. When considered in terms of the physical world they represent the four main densities of matter—Earth relates to solids, Water to liquids, Air to gasses, and Fire to energy. In human terms, we see reflected the fourfold constitution of man—Earth the body, Water the soul (feelings), Air the mind, and Fire the heart (spirit). In terms of Jungian Psychology, the elements correlate to the four perceptual modes—Earth to sensation, Water to feeling, Air to thinking, and Fire to intuition. In interpersonal terms they correlate to the four types of love—Earth to *sex*, the attraction of the body; Water to *eros*, the oceanic urge to merge; Air to *philia,* brotherly love and friendship; and Fire to *agape,* selfless love in the religious or non-possessive romantic sense.

In more occult terms we see represented the idea of the different vibratory levels and planes of reality which correspond to the fourfold constitution of man—Earth the material, physical plane, Water the astral or desire plane, Air the causal or mental plane, and Fire the spiritual plane. The symbolism implied in these images helps us to visualize how different vibratory levels are thought to coexist simultaneously in the same time/space locus, for we can see how soil, water, air, and energy can exist together in the same moment and place. We perceive the dense physical level with our five senses because they are tuned to that particular vibratory wavelength, although there have always been those with more finely tuned senses who could detect the more subtle, refined aspects of the physical world, such as the energy fields which surround all life forms. Likewise is the astral plane apprehended through the feelings—this is how we have vague hunches and sense things about other persons (especially those with whom there is an emotional connection) and is the source of dreams, symbolic visions, and psychic impressions.

Through the mind we "see" on the causal plane—in mental concentration and cessation of attention to sensory input we become aware of another place which is not only of our own creation, but exists objectively as well. Great thinkers do not simply dream up the truths they express—they discover them in the same way an explorer discovers something on the physical plane. And it is through the heart that we experience the spiritual plane of life. By giving of ourselves and following the intuitive promptings of the spirit we escape the prison of the isolated ego and truly *experience* the being of another and the essence of life itself.

This concept teaches a very important lesson—that the ideal and heavenly worlds do not exist elsewhere, apart from the worlds of form and concrete reality, but are *right here and right now,* permeating everything and lying hidden to the senses behind the factual realities which they animate. We do not have to wait until our bodies die to go to heaven—we are already there and need only to realize it by raising the vibratory level of our consciousness. We can have heaven on earth if we are willing to work for it. This is the reason we seek to view the physical in a symbolic rather than a literal fashion (although both have their place).

Once we learn to see *through* things in this way symbols such as Tarot cards or astrological glyphs come to life and begin to reveal their secrets to us, much to our benefit.

When applied to the Xultan images, the symbolism of the four elements works differently in each of the three main divisions of the cards. Since the Lower Arcana as a whole deals mainly with outer life, the elements applied to this level describe the types of external experiences that are available. The numbered cards describe the archetypal situations and conditions of existence, while the court cards describe the different types of people one may encounter and their roles in life. Since the Higher Arcana deal more with the inner life, the elements describe the different levels on which one experiences and develops himself and help to typify the milestones of this process.

The elements apply to the suits of the Lower Arcana in this way: Earth correlates to Jades, Water to Cups, Air to Swords, and Fire to Staffs. These are superimposed upon, and combined with the seasonal correlations to give the suits added meaning. The symbols for the individual signs of each element will be found on the court cards of each suit—the first four, or primordial signs on the Lords, the second four, or individual signs on the Ladies, and the last four, or universal signs on the Servants. In other words, the glyphs for the three Fire signs are found on the Lord, Lady, and Servant of Staffs, those of the three Water signs on the Lord, Lady, and Servant of Cups, and so on. The Warrior of each suit corresponds to that element as a whole and carries no individual sign. It is interesting to note that the suits which correlate to the odd-numbered signs—the Fire and Air signs, which are considered to be positively polarized (expressive, active, dynamic, etc.) have symbols which are male/phallic in nature, whereas the suits which correlate to the even-numbered signs—the Earth and Water signs, which are considered negatively polarized (retentive, receptive, stable, etc.) have symbols which are female/vaginal in nature.

It is necessary to caution one against over-literalness in the interpretations of the symbols assigned to the court cards. The Lady of Cups doesn't necessarily represent "a Scorpio" (a person whose sun-sign is Scorpio). It signifies a person who exhibits the qualities symbolized by the sign Scorpio within the context

of a given situation. The same person could be shown by different cards in different readings depending upon their role in that situation. A more detailed knowledge of sign and personality typology would be helpful to the person who is seriously interested in gaining skill in this area.

When we turn to the cards of the Higher Arcana, we encounter the feature of the Xultun deck that most radically departs from and enlarges upon the foundation of the past. I remember early 1976, when I would drive across town to the Bodhi Tree bookstore in West L.A. and would stop by the art gallery on La Cienega where Peter worked on the way back to my apartment in Silverlake. He was at that time involved in painting the picture of the Higher Arcana and I remember how struck I was by the intuitive rightness of the unified concept and by the fact that the conception took place at the Winter solstice of 1975, a year that was so significant to occultists. I consider this regeneration and reorganization of these archetypes of the inner planes to be altogether fitting in an age where the value and importance of subjective growth and experience is being rediscovered.

I have yet to encounter a method of correlating astrological symbols to the individual cards which satisfies me (although I recommend that the reader make up his own mind on the subject), but when we assemble the cards into the whole picture we see represented most clearly the hierarchy of levels symbolized by the astrollogical concept of the elements. The bottom level corresponds to the Earth/physical and like the Jades is colored green, the second level to the Water/emotional and is blue like the Cups, the third to the Air/mental and is yellow like the Swords, the fourth to the Fire/spiritual and is red like the Staffs. The cards at the very top may be part of the spiritual level, or may refer to a fifth element long rumored about in astrological circles—Ether.

Up to this point we have approached the Tarot through Astrology from a theoretical, philosophical, meditative standpoint, largely ignoring its specific, practical, dynamic aspect—that of divination. This is the aspect of the Tarot which is far more fascinating to the average person of common sense than dry intellectual discourses. He does not want to buy an expensive pack of cards simply to look at and think about and put away in a drawer somewhere—he wants to do something with them, use them, make them a part of his life. This is easily understood. It is no coincidence, however, that this is also the side of the Tarot with which serious scholars have had the most embarrassment and contempt. This is also understandable when we see how this practice is usually conducted—with the shallowest and most venal of motives, where memorized lists of stale, rigid interpretations substitute for true understanding, where a fatalistic philosophy divorces the inner from the outer life by presupposing that events just "happen to" the individual, who is a passive, powerless spectator in the whole drama. This is the antithesis of a creative use of the cards because it enslaves rather than frees us. What good does it do us to know that we are going to receive a large sum of money or that we are going to experience the breakup of a close personal relationship unless we understand what we have done or what is in us that is causing it to happen and how we can influence these events? Are we to resign ourselves to impotence in the face of all powerful fate? This philosphy blinds us to the fact that our attitudes and reactions to events are every bit as important as the nature of the event itself. Is inheriting a large sum of money to be considered good luck if it allows us to indulge a weakness in our character that heretofore went

unnourished? Is the breakup of a marriage to be considered a misfortune if it teaches us to stand on our own feet and helps us to become stronger and more successful? We can see why a deep psychological and philosphical understanding of oneself and the symbols one is working with constitutes a necesssary prerequisite for attempting to do card readings in a helpful and responsible manner. Only with such an understanding can a person apply divination with any positive results. Given such a basis, however, divination becomes the inseparable compliment to meditation, and the ivory tower attitude of intellectuals becomes inexcusable because it has the same result as ignorant fatalism—it divorces the inner life from outer experience. Practicing divination allows the spontaneous events of life to teach us the meanings of symbols beyond what any preconceived notions can do. It allows us to test what we have learned, for all too often in practical application one learns that the theories of authorities sound great on paper but simply do not work. And the self-discovery and knowledge that comes from a thorough meditative study of the symbols is complimented by the self-discipline and development that comes from applying and working through these insights.

I would therefore make the following suggestions to the aspiring cartomancer, advice grounded in the experience of years of study and professional practice of various symbolic arts. First, make a thorough study of this book and any others on the subject which may seem worthwhile. Acquire knowledge in related areas of study. Study the cards themselves and let the pictures speak directly to you and suggest meanings that you may not find in books. Get to know every card so well that the meaning of each one becomes internalized and an intuitive feeling develops. Make your deck your own—sleep with it under your pillow, carry it around, get it out often, study it, handle it, use it. Be persevering, for the process I spoke of in the first paragraph takes time.

For the student with some background in Astrology, I would recommend trying the horoscope method of laying out the cards. It is especially useful in doing psychological character analysis readings and expositions of the general state of the various departments of the persons' life, although other spreads are more useful for answering specific questions or predicting the course of events. It is done in this way: after concentrating on the subject, shuffling and cutting the deck, lay out twelve cards counter-clockwise in a circle starting from the extreme left hand point. Each card corresponds to one of the astrological houses by which all of the facets of experience are categorized. Here is a summary of the meanings of each house:

1st: The person and their attitude towards their self, their personality (window or mask towards the world), how they naturally take action and approach to life.

2nd: What they value, what they own or possess, their income, money, the pleasure they derive from their possessions and their body.

3rd: How they think and learn, what they are interested in, how and what they communicate, their neighbors and siblings, transportation and short travels.

4th: Their home, family and domestic life, early childhood influences, roots and foundation, land and property.

5th: Their creative self-expression, art, pleasure and recreation, romance and love, sports, children, hobbies, performances.

6th: Their work and daily routine, diet, hygiene, health or lack thereof, service, relationships with servants.

7th: Their relationships with others of equal status, cooperative ventures and partnerships, the spouse, open enemies.

8th: Their participation in shared resources (bank, etc.), emotional relationships, sex, death, crises and transitions, legacies.

9th: Their self-expansion in the form of distant travels, higher education, philosphy, religion, the law and courts of law, publicity.

10th: Career, status, reputation, ambitions, achievements, honors, relationships with bosses and authority figures.

11th: Their friends, associates, casual acquaintenances, social connections, clubs, groups, hopes and wishes.

12th: Their secrets, private affairs, skeletons in th closet, spiritual experiences, meditation, confinement and isolation.

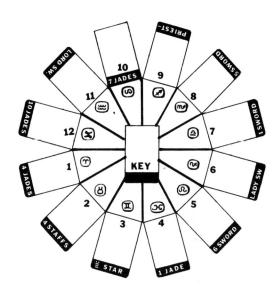

Here is a brief example of a reading done by this method. The cards fell as follows: 1—4 Jades, 2—4 Staffs, 3—The Star, 4—Ace Jades, 5—6 Swords, 6—Lady Swords, 7—Ace Swords, 8—5 Swords, 9—The Priest, 10—7 Jades (reversed), 11—Lord Swords, 12—10 Jades. The person considers himself practical, strong, dependable, and worthwhile. He comes on slowly and carefully. He values things of beauty, art objects, is joyous and pleasure loving, likes easy money. He studies life and talks incessantly about his experiences in the world and what he has learned from them. He lives in an expensive home and invests money in real estate. His hobby is studying and experimenting with science, his children are helpful but competitive. His work involves socializing, perhaps art, and he gets along well with those under him. He has great difficulty in partnerships because he demands his own way and has to be the boss. He has many fights and quarrels in his emotional relationships and may have sexual hangups. He is intensely religious, and if travelling to a foreign country would prefer to visit religious shrines and monuments. He has so far not been successful in achieving his career ambitions. He enjoys associating with persons who are well informed and good conversationalists. He may have a lot of money hidden away.

This is a very ordinary, mechanical reading of the type that requires no psychic inspiration and which anybody could do with a little practice. It does not illustrate counseling technique, which is an important part of reading for others and is the method by which we determine the correct interpretation from several possibilities. For example, when reading the Ace of Jades in the fourth house we do not tell him what it means—we ask him if he came from a wealthy family. It turns out that he did not know his parents and grew up in an orphanage. We ask him if he owns an expensive home. He replies that he does, that it is comfortable if not ostentatious and gives him a

feeling of being firmly rooted. We ask him if he owns land or property other than his home. His eyebrows raise. We ask him if he has money invested in real estate. He replies that he has just recently made a sizeable investment. We tell him that it looks like a sound one and go on to the fifth house. Through counseling technique we open up the other person and establish the cross flow of energy that makes for good readings. Just remember that the cards show the potentials and principles in operation and the purpose of divining them is to help the person guide their expression and not to impress them with our skill in telling fortunes. Avoid dogmatic statements.

The student will learn to trust and be guided by what his experience teaches him and not to rely too heavily on book interpretations. There are many good reasons for this. For one, the written literature on the Tarot is for the most part hopelessly corrupt, made so on the one hand by esotericists who, true to their kind, claim to fear releasing secret knowledge to the public (who are not ready for the truth) and so, by their odd logic, prefer to disseminate half truths, vague references, and outright lies; and on the other hand by authors of the derivative type who, having no experience or under-

standing of their own, copy indiscriminately from both wise and worthless authorities and thus perpetuate confusion and misunderstanding. Many prominent authorities on the subject wrote near the turn of the century and their ideas are more valid for their own era than for ours. They tend to indulge in fatalism and the dualistic style of thinking which sees some cards as totally good and others as totally bad, rather than seeing the positive and negative possibilities in every card. What is left for the person who receives a totally negative reading—suicide? The Tarot is largely based upon the principle of synchronicity, and a reading is a product of that unique moment in time. Seeing through the eyes of the dead blinds us to the now. While the experience of others can point us in the right direction, it is no substitute for acquiring our own. I would only caution the student to be aware of his limitations and lack of experience while he is learning and avoid giving the impression of great attainment. This attitude of modesty will open many doors of itself and will free one from the burdensome pressure of trying to live up to the unrealistic expectations of others.

We are all limited by the amount of innate talent we bring to the pursuit of any art, but the proper discipline will develop whatever talent we may have to the fullest. It goes without saying that those who are most psychically gifted will be most successful at Tarot reding—those who have the Water signs or the 4th, 8th, and 12th houses strongly tenanted in their charts and/or have the Moon, Neptune, and Pluto prominently placed and aspecting one another. The Fire types are also good at seeing into the potentials of situations but don't seem to be as adept at picking up impressions from others. Aspects from the psychic or intuitive planets to Mercury help the person to formulate what he is dimly aware of and communicate it to others.

Jung said that the future can be told because events are prepared in the unconscious long before they work their way into manifestation. Symbols can help us to gain access to levels where events are in the process of being born, while they are still potential and can to some extent be shaped and influenced. The value of this kind of insight does not need to be emphasized. Through such insight we can become participants in the creation of our lives rather than being the pawns of forces and drives of whose existence we are not even aware, let alone understand. Symbols are also the key to

levels where we ourselves are in the process of being born, where the man or woman of tomorrow exists here and now in the form of the seed. The question to you, dear Fool, is this—do you have what it takes to face yourself in this mirror and see who you really are, to step through the looking-glass to the other side? Undreamed of terrors and wonders await you. The tools are before you, the path begins at your feet.

What will be your answer?

Tarot and

There is an ancient Indian tradition that connects the days of the month to the parts of the human body, and so by extension the Tarot cards can be placed in the same positions. There would be a use for such a system in enquiries regarding health matters. The card representing the particular part of the body under enquiry could be used as the key card.

There is also an old astrological tradition that does the same thing, the astrological correlations are listed along with the appropriate Higher Arcana card. They are quite different. The Maya simply started numbering on the right side of the body and proceeded over to the left side. In the chart opposite the right side of the body is represented by the female figure and the left side by the male figure. There is only one palce where the cards do not relate to both sexes, and that is card 21, the Earth card. This is placed on the womb, although it does serve both sexes when dealing with body fluids.

Card (•) is placed on the right leg and it represents all of the parts of the leg, the toes, arch, heel, the ankle, calf, thigh, knee and any of the bones, muscles and ligaments connected with the right leg.

Card (••) is the heart, the throne of the blood as the Maya call it. This card also governs the venal and artery system throughout the whole body.

Card (•••) governs the lungs and all of those parts immediately connected with the utilization of air as a food for the body.

Card (••••) governs the mouth, the teeth, and those muscles used in swallowing.

Card (▬) is the right hand, including thumb and fingers, the wrist, elbow, and the entire arm.

Card (▬•) is the right ear. The organ of hearing on that side, it also includes the ear lobe.

Card (▬••) is in charge of the throat, the muscles of the neck, and organs of speech such as vocal cords.

Card (▬•••) represents the right eye, all of its associated parts including the eye socket, lid and the muscles that control that eye.

Card (▬••••) the head including the skull, brain, hair and forehead.

Card (▬▬) the left eye and all of its parts.

Card (▬▬•) the nose, septum, nostrils, and the sense of smell.

Card (▬▬••) the left ear and all of its parts.

Card (▬▬•••) the spinal column, from the base of the skull to the sacroiliac.

Card (▬▬••••) the tongue and its muscles, including the sense of taste.

Card (▬▬▬) the left hand, fingers, thumb, arm and elbow.

Card (▬▬▬•) the kidney and bladder systems.

Card (▬▬▬••) the stomach, the digestive organs, etc.

Card (▬▬▬•••) the anus, colon, and associated muscles.

Card (▬▬▬••••) the left foot, toes, ankle, and leg, etc.

ne Body's Parts:

Card (▤) the genitals and reproductive system.

Card (▤) the womb in women and the lymphatic fluid system throughout the body of both sexes.

There are other parts of the body not listed here, but it is easy enough to see how they would attach to one or other of the cards. It is not advised that the cards be used to solve a medical problem, in such cases the questioner should be advised to seek help from a medical doctor. The cards may be used to divine possible outcomes, relationships, and the like.

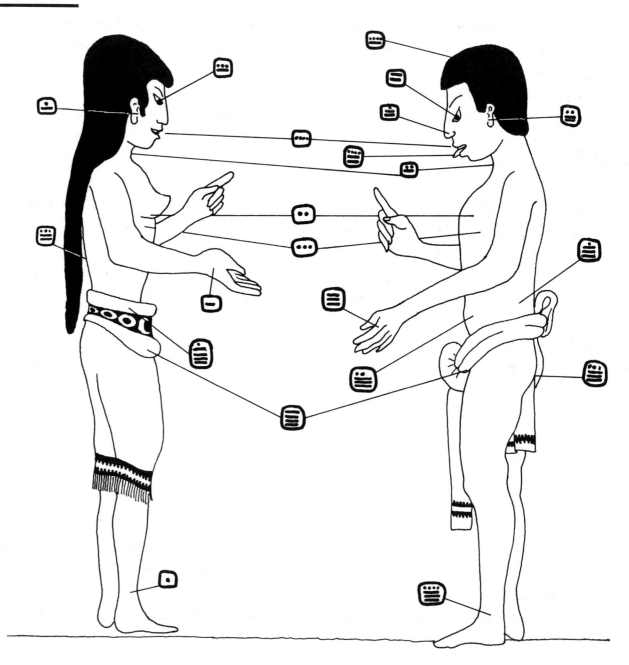

The Higher Arcana:

The Tarot deck divides into three decks, the higher arcana, which has twenty-two cards, the court cards which number sixteen and form a bridge between the higher and the lower arcana, which numbers forty cards.

The word arcana means mysteries, or hidden things. Its singular form is arcanum. The higher arcana is not meant to imply that these mysteries are in some way superior to the lower ones. The terms higher and lower, or sometimes major and minor, refer to the subject matter dealt with in the cards. The lower arcana treats with the everyday occurrences in our lives, the mundane, the method of earning a living, and our interactions with others in the way we live our lives. The higher arcana treats with the underlying motivations, the psychological and spiritual movements within our lives.

Tarot cards first made their appearance in Europe somewhere in the tenth or eleventh century. A great deal of time has been used and a lot of research done to uncover the origins of tarot, but of little avail. The consensus of opinion seems to favour a Chinese origin for the cards. China was the only country to use cards of any sort.

In eighteenth century France the idea became popular that the cards had their origin in Egypt; this is now known not to be so. No mention of cards has ever been found in the extensive writings of that civilization. One other point to be made is that the zero card (the Fool) could not have existed in Egypt as there was no knowledge of a concept of zero. And Tarot without the Fool is unthinkable, for it is the principal card in the deck, so much so that when gambling became a popular pastime, the whole of the higher arcana was abandoned, except for the Fool cards which survives as the Joker.

The Chinese cards were related to the I CHING, and were arranged in four suits called, coins, tens of coins, hundreds of coins and thousands of coins. It is interesting that in several decks of tarot the lower arcana has a suit called coins, which are always the Earth cards, diamonds in ordinary playing cards.

The earliest recorded Tarot decks in Europe seem to have appeared in Italy; it is thought in a little town not too far from Venice, called Piedemonte. This town happens to be in a valley through which the Tarot River flows. No one knows if this is a coincidence or what, for no one knows the meaning of the word tarot. It is thought that perhaps it is an anagram for the word ROTA, which is Italian and means wheel. In ordinary playing cards there is the suit of spades; this comes from the Italian word for sword which is spade.

Those who cling to the idea of an Egyptian origin for the cards think that tarot is a corruption of the word THOTH who was the Egyptian god of wisdom and science. He is thought to have been the inventor of speech and letters, and the protector of the arts. Thoth kept the records of judgment in the hall of Osiris. Usually he is shown with the head of an ibis or a dog. The Greek god with the same attributes was Hermes. However, no matter how attractive this idea is, there is no verification available at all.

The most logical explanation is that the cards were brought from China by one of the early Venetian travelers, for they had made trips to China since Roman days. The grandfather of Marco Polo, brought back to Italy the idea of paper money, and that is not such a long stretch to include playing cards.

At various times in the cards' history the church has attempted to ban the lower arcana, but with little success. There has never been any attempt to suppress the higher arcana.

Many legends have grown up around the cards, and the character of the Fool was used as the hero in many medieval dramas. The knight in the King Arthur legend, Sir Galahad, whose strength was as the strength of ten, because his heart was pure, was the Fool, in his search for the Holy Grail (cup containing the blood of Christ).

The character Parsifal in the German legends, set to music by Richard Wagner, was modeled on the Fool. The search for the Grail is, of course, a hidden way of saying the search for enlightenment.

In medieval times great care had to be exercised in the expounding of such ideas, for the Knights Templar had been attacked and totally desimated by the Christian Church, whose legal arm, the Inquisition, had gained such a bloodthirsty reputation throughout the centuries it was in operation. Records show that over two million people were put to death by the courts of the inquisitors, proving beyond any doubt that Christianity never had a monolithic hold upon the populations of Europe.

There is one theory about the origin of the cards that relates directly to the Knights Templar. Knowing that the end was close, the knights decided to put all of their knowledge down in a form that would reveal and hide at the same time. Legend says that they made the first tarot cards for this purpose.

Unfortunately, no concrete evidence has ever been found to back up this idea.

Thousands of variations upon the tarot deck exist, almost every nation has its version of the cards. There are very complex philosphical systems attached to the cards. A popular one is the joining of the Kabbalah, a Hebrew system of knowledge to the higher arcana. The Hebrew alphabet has twenty-two letters and each has a complex value system which in turn is attached to the twenty-two cards of the Higher Arcana.

The Fool

ZERO

DESCRIPTION: A young person of indeterminate sex, stands in the mouth of a Jaguar, the left hand raised as though doubtful or unseeing. In the right hand a simple white flower with six petals. On the head is a dress of green feathers out of which protrudes a rather animated skull in profile. Other aspects of the headdress are various ribbons, a water lily bud and a canoe like decoration on the front, below which is a circle with a dot in its center. Above the Fool is a bright white light, and behind him

to the left of the card, the upper portion of the sun's disk. In front of the Jaguar's jaw, on the plinth of the Sorcerer's platform, is the figure of an old man navigating a canoe in which sits a fish. The other passengers appear in the next card.

INTERPRETATION: The Fool is represented as a person who seems unable to pay attention to himself or the things around him. It is the average state of most of us in our present behavior, manifesting little wisdom, apathetic to the world about us, and seemingly victims of circumstances. As we are all full of potential, so is the Fool. Children and fools tell the truth, and this naievete (innocence) is the breath, the energy source which propels the Fool inevitably forward on the journey to the knowledge of the Sorcerer.

SIGNIFICANCE: The Fool manifests the first unconscious act of a separate self, breath. The card represents the Spirit of a thing, its primary essence, its nature, its causal expression. The person who is ruled by their stars, but manifests a natural curiosity, not the curiosity of a scientist (that will come) but the tinkering

enquiry of a child where play becomes discovery.

INVERTED: The play now assumes a purpose and has become work. Discovery has gone and given place to *SEARCH FOR DISCOVERIES.* The breath becomes suppressed and controlled, circumstances begin to exert pressure. Expectations are built and will inevitably give way to disappointments. The Fool develops *INTENTIONS*, and the seeking assumes *GOALS. BELIEFS* take the place of the naivete and innocence becomes a tool with which to manipulate knowing.

SEXUAL EXPRESSION: The Fool is that desire, that movement (spirit) within each person that compells one towards some expression of, or response to the sexual urge. It does not represent the response, but indicates the direction of the response. Sexually the card is a neuter, for the Fool has not yet a role or a model, has no heroes and represents that pre-pubescent stage just before sexual identification takes place, that stage when affection can move in any direction to express itself in sexual gratification. The card will point out the object of desire and the manner in which sex will manifest itself.

VALUE: Breath.   COLOR: Pale Yellow.
TONE: E-Natural   DIRECTION: None.

MEANING: The Fool represents to his own person the *NAGUAL.* To himself he is the unknown. He is caught in the belief he can know himself, he thinks that the mind can know the mystery of existence, and so the search begins. At first the Fool just wanders aimlessly through the jungle of the mind picking up bits and pieces of information. Gradually this accretion begins to assume significance, and he gets the feeling he knows where he is going, various paths seem to lead him to important crossroads. He asks himself seemingly significant questions, "Who am I? Where am I going? What is the reason for existing? What is life all about? What is relationship?" He questions everyone and everything, and the more he questions, the less he understands. Everyone he questions is only too willing to supply him with answers, yet none of the answers satisfy him. He boils with discontent, for he has this driving urge to find the unknown, reality, God. His mind only responds to this search to understand the unknowable, to partake of the body of God. He wants to return home. He dreams of happiness and joy,

and he is willing to do anything to achieve this most worthy goal. He will leave no question unanswered, no stone unturned, he will enquire into every system of philosophy, he will ask every wise man, every saint, all of whom will point the way, and none of whom will he believe. He will take up social reform, will shout highly admirable political slogans. He will work for the good of mankind. He will build political parties and healing institutions, but still he does not know the self, the reality, the unknown, God. He must try harder! He does, he tries harder, and at last he's got it! He knows, at last he has it, the mind is silent and he knows it. At last he loves everyone, and he knows it. He knows happiness and can at last point the way to others—yet? No! No! He is really happy, has he not escaped at last, the turmoil, the pain, the confusion of life? Has he not at last discovered the secret of life, the divine and permanent security? Well has he not? Then in the flash of a lack of thought he saw it, what a marvellous refuge he had built, what a marvellous escape! WHAT A FOOL HE IS!

URANUS: This is the planet of the unexpected. At its best aspect, it can give rise to genius, more often however it gives an indication of erratic behavior. The Uranian is both unique and original. Usually they are able and original in their chosen field, they have integrity and an inner purpose that is hard to defeat. Those ruled by this planet want to achieve in a practical manner, they manifest ability to predict the shape of things to come. Badly aspected, Uranus can produce eccentricity akin to madness, revolutionaries, misfits and those who make a fetish of unconventional behavior. They also tend to be reckless and accident-prone.

URANUS RULES: House of Aquarius
DAY: Morning.
PLANTS: Fennel; Rhubarb; Valerian; English Oak; Holly.
BODY: Nervous system.
METAL: Aluminum
FLOWER: Clover, Oxalis.

The Sorcerer

DESCRIPTION: A powerful looking man, standing on his toes as though leaning on the wind. His right hand holds high above his head, a magical wand made of seven jade rings. Supported on his left shoulder and held by his left hand is a plain wooden staff upon which is a still living leaf. Around his waist is an elaborate belt, decorated with two large tasseled masks. His headdress and collar are very elaborate affairs. Above him is the same white light as appears in the Fool card. On the left side of the

card to the Sorcerer's right is an almost perfectly shaped mountain. He stands on a high platform on which is also an empty cup. On the side of the platform continues the design that began in the previous card, a canoe in which sits a monkey, the Fool, a parrot and a jaguar. The canoe is being rowed by a young man seated on its bow.

INTERPRETATION: The Sorcerer is represented as a person secure in himself, open to whatever opportunities present themselves, and able to avail himself of them. This person is not swayed by his dreams or fantasies, he knows *WHAT IS.* He has no desires that cannot be fulfilled, knows how self functions, and is able to work creatively within its limitations. The Sorcerer has brought all the facets of his being into balance, and so it manifests as power and the ability to manage things on a material level. He is the Fool at the end of his journey.

SIGNIFICANCE: The Sorcerer manifests the principal of *UNITY,* the origin of which is unknowable to the human consciousness. His upright attitude shows the *WILL* that *PROCEEDS INTO ACTION.* The Sorcerer, as the

word implies, stands at the source of the unknown, seeing it, feeling it, using it, but never able to explain it, he manifests the unknown in the known. The Sorcerer is a light to others, and never seeks to know why. He *MANIFESTS.*

INVERTED: The intellect is flawed and shows itself in intellectual pursuits, becoming skillful at building traps for others, displaying itself in guile and subtle practices of ego. The Sorcerer's power is inept and used for destructive and self-aggrandising ends. He becomes a master at explaining life to *LESSER BEINGS.* He becomes willful. His creative abilities do not show themselves on the material level, but in the realm of *IDEAS.*

SEXUAL EXPRESSION: The Sorcerer enjoys a life of sexual balance, although this may not be apparent to the casual observer, for it may fluctuate between periods of celibacy and hypersexuality. During the periods of sexual expression, the Sorcerer nature becomes very appealing to both sexes and may express itself in bisexual practices. The *UNITY* and *BALANCE* within this very accomplished person shows itself externally (whether male or female) as a sexually active, youthful, vigorous individual, displaying the most desirable qualities of their sex.

VALUE: Intellect.
COLOR: Bright Yellow.   TONE: E-Natural.
DIRECTION: Above.

THE ACE CARDS OF THE LOWER ARCANA ARE THE ELEMENTAL EXPRESSIONS OF THE SORCERER'S BEING: THEY ARE HIS FOUR TOOLS OF RENEWAL.

With the 1 of Staffs his spirit creates and
  supports.
With the 1 of Cups his emotion preserves
  and refreshes.
With the 1 of Swords his mind divides and
  silences.
With the 1 of Jades his body redeems and
  rewards.

MEANING: What a Fool he was, this Sorcerer! In seeing the foolishness of his actions, the Sorcerer stumbled into the light of truth, he had kept himself so busy considering what it was that drove him on in his quest, that he never had time to enquire into his confusion, his strife and the antagonism, all the foolish things that were his view of life. When foolishness is gone, then intelligence can shine forth. The Fool who is stupid and wants to become intelligent is still a fool with foolish wants. Stupidity can never be made into wisdom; only when stupidity ceases is there wisdom and intelligence. The Fool tried very hard to *BECOME* intelligent, and obviously could not, he was able to fake it, but that did not make him happy. The first act of *SORCERY* that took place was the seeing. The Fool did not see, he was stupid, he could not see. Seeing that he was foolish took place and the Sorcerer was born. The Fool stopped being a fool and the Sorcerer was there. The Sorcerer is greater than the known of the Fool which urged him ever on toward an unknown. It is the Sorcerer that sees what it is in the Fool that created his confusion, his pursuit of fame and accumulation of knowledge. The Sorcerer sees what made the Fool want to escape through art and music. With the throwing off of the known, the unknown was experienced and the Sorcerer came about. The Sorcerer is not the product of the mind, but that which happens when the mind is silent, when it no longer creates a future where it hopes to fulfill itself. The Sorcerer does not seek the unknown, but understands the accumulative processes of the mind which are forever within the known, the organized and the understood. The Sorcerer is constantly at attention, constantly aware, without distraction, without identification and without condemnation. He does not seek the unknown (God) but searches to understand the confusion and misery in himself, for in that work, joy comes into being and fulfillment is continuous.

MERCURY: This planet has a special relationship with young people; when it is prominent, that person has a youthful quality that always remains regardless of age. Mercury can be chameleon-like and volatile, rising and falling rapidly in response to circumstances. These natives make superior critics, lawyers, scientists, writers, and journalists. Usually these people of Mercury are logical, cogent in speech and writing, quick and accurate. Badly aspected they are shrewd and guileful, and don't submit to mental exercise, they can be unprincipaled, argumentative, mean and sly. They can be clever, tricky and deceitful.

MERCURY RULES: House of Gemini.
DAY: Wednesday.
PLANTS: Aniseed Caraway; Carrots; Celery;
  Dill; Flax; Grasses; Linseed; Mulberry;
  Oats; Parsley.
BODY: The mind. The memory. The power of
  speech, arms, hands and fingers.
METAL: Quick Silver.
FLOWER: Jasmine, Honeysuckle.

The Priestess ● ●

IMIX   In the womb ··· 2

DESCRIPTION: An attractive woman sits under a canopy and holds in her left hand a screen-fold book. It is the map of the Fool's journey. With her right hand she points out stars which may guide him. In front and on the Priestess's right are two small pillars, one black and one white. In front of the black pillar and protruding out of the Warrior card below is his starry banner. The canopy has an ornamental comb on the roof; the comb is painted green and is decorated with two pairs of eyes. Below

the straw roof are written four glyphs: shield/jaguar, on high, woman speaks (softly?), dark (old?) waning moon. There are other glyphs on the base of the canopy. Some are readable, others are not, yet the sense of them is not clear. What looks to be wisteria entwines the canopy. There are many stars in the sky. Seven of them are large and bright and are probably planets.

INTERPRETATION: The Priestess is presented as a person whose attention is concentrated, though somewhat divided. She seems to have just recalled something important. The Priestess represents consciousness. She is the content of the mind, arranged between the two pillars of the mind, that which she recognizes (ego) and that unrecognized, dark part called the unconscious. The woman on this card is the inspirer of the dreams and visions that reveal the existence of life beyond our conscious perception.

SIGNIFICANCE: The Priestess manifests memory, that absolutely necessary component in the construction of an ego. Information is stored in the brain in opposites for easy recall.

That which gives the mind pleasure and gratification is called positive, good, I. That which gives it pain and anguish is called negative, bad, the other. Conscious, unconscious; right, wrong; approve, disapprove; indifference, concern; like, dislike; WHITE, BLACK. The human brain is an organizing instrument. It strives to bring about order.

INVERTED: Because of the tension resulting from this constant friction of opposites, the lazy personality selects for itself a negative atttitude. It develops a passive opposition to others, sinks into self-pity, becomes grasping and self motivated. The mind cloaks itself in obscurity, to cover its failure to use memory in a constructive and mind-expanding way. It may rely on drugs, hoping they will bring it harmony and heal the division already too deep to be affected by anything other than concentrated effort and work.

SEXUAL EXPRESSION: The Priestess is the feminine aspect within each person (especially men), the anima, that primal image that endows us with intuition and a sense of magic. This card represents the perfect woman all men dream about and all women wish to be. To the Fool she is the "older woman," who opens sexual responses he did not know existed and ensures sexual fulfillment of both mind and body. The Priestess has the power to use and abuse the Fool. For her, where sex is concerned, sin does not exist.

VALUE: Memory.
COLOR: Blue. TONE: G-Sharp. A-Flat.
DIRECTION: Below.

MEANING: This is the first encounter of the Fool on his journey toward the knowledge of the Sorcerer. He is barely aware, perceiving only dimly his involvement in the opposites and is hardly concerned with their operation. The Priestess demonstrates to the Fool that it is here, within the womb of memory, that polarity (the opposites) is formed and the ego is born. It is from the tension between what the Fool sees as the positive and negative aspects of existence, that the ego derives its energy, its life, and its form. In the womb of memory the ego has its birth. It is the interaction of the polarities that gives rise to all the concepts according to a value system deemed superior to all others. This operation allows the individual to indulge in the illusion of separateness. The two pairs of eyes on the shelter over the Priestess are symbols of the two worlds the Fool inhabits: illusion, that which he likes,

singles out, and calls reality; and the choiceless awareness that brings understanding of WHAT IS, the true perception of reality. The Fool sees that he is divided and thinks himself incapable of functioning in an integrated manner. This card is an expression of the division that is within us all. It offers the Fool no hope of overcoming this situation. The movement within the Fool is to select one aspect or the other, to create a sense of security, but the more he does this the greater is the pressure for recognition from the neglected aspect. With effort and work the Fool sees that everything on this planet, perhaps in all the universe, is constructed in this very manner. There is a negative and positive part, a male and a female part, and one part does not function well without the other. It seems that all energy, perhaps the life-force itself, derives its essence from this tension between the opposites. The Fool thinks that if one thing is true and valid, its opposite must be untrue and invalid.

MOON: The Moon represents the self that one shows to the world. A well-placed moon is the best indicator of a pleasing and popular personality. A bad lunar placement may point to personality problems, and other people may not form good opinions of such a person. The moon's postition shows the type of position ordinary people occupy in their everyday life. With outstanding or famous people, it governs the image they manifest in public.

MOON RULES: House of Cancer.
DAY: Monday.
PLANTS: Beans, bananas, cabbage family, cucumbers, comfrey, lettuce, melons, mushrooms, pumpkin, sugarcane, succulents, violets, watercress, willow.
BODY: Left eye, body fluids, digestion, all sense impressions—sight, hearing, touch, taste, and smell.
METAL: Silver.
FLOWER: Lily.

 # The Consort ●●●

IK   Born of air ·································· 3

behind which is seen a large portion of the rising sun. She is the Consort, the companion of the ruler. Between her and the sun can be seen flying two sinister, vulture-like birds, possibly the opposites of the previous card.

INTERPRETATION: The Consort is a title born equally by either sex and implies a complimentary function. A Consort receives strength from the Ruler and in return aids in carrying the weight of office. It is a fruitful and creative position, often responsible for projects involving the arts and sciences. A successful Consort exhibits balance and stability and an openness that deals fairly with all. The Consort stands for the perception and birth of new ideas, as well as the birth of children.

SIGNIFICANCE: The Consort represents new life. She is the ruler of the earth paradise, the earth mother. She brings about spiritual awakening through a devotion to physical work and creative pursuits. It is the birth of a third principal, that of conciliation between the opposites, that makes a work of art possible; but really it is the work (labor) itself that is the conciliation between the destructive and crea-

tive parts, and it is this which gives a work of art its power.

INVERTED: The influence exerted on the Ruler by the Consort becomes manipulation, and instability results. More and more she saps the strength from its source, unbalancing the partnership, disrupting the home and leading it toward inevitable destruction.

SEXUAL EXPRESSION: A person with the Consort's nature chooses their own sexual partners and is the instigator of the union. In a spread the card denotes initiative in all aspects of sexual expression. It predicts fertility and rich harvests in the act itself. It promises successful courtships, bountiful foreplay, and intercourse. Inverted, the card inclines the Consort to doubt about ability to function , resorting to inventive excuses to avoid the act. It can indicate infidelity.

VALUE: Reaction.
COLOR: Green.   TONE: F-Sharp. G-Flat.
DIRECTION: East.

DESCRIPTION: An attractive middle-aged woman sits very erect upon a seat over which is draped the skin of a jaguar. She wears an elaborate headdress that comes down over her shoulders and forms the jaw of a serpent, through which she looks steadfastly forward. Tucked under her left arm is a shield, and in that hand she holds two darts very close together and the same color. Her right hand is raised in a gesture that seems to say: quiet, relax. Her seat is on a very elaborate dais,

MEANING: The Consort presents to the Fool the possibility of resolving the tension between the opposites by the birth of a third, conciliatory principal. Until this moment the Fool had only seen the world in dualistic terms, that is, as good or bad, right or wrong. He had been conscious only of images as they came and went, so it is not surprising that he was unconscious of *existing,* which *is* reality and which has three dimensions. The Fool was only conscious of that within himself, which was illusion, and he was unconscious of that in which he was real. The Fool had struggled to be positive, to be for life and to avoid death; he searched for beauty and avoided ugliness, held to truth and eschewed error. He wanted to create and not to destroy. How could his search for good only bring him sorrow? "Wait! Slow down, Fool. Why do you hold to the positive alone?" demands the Consort. "I seek goodness, beauty, truth and iight, because I see these qualities help me survive and I want to live. I have a drive, a will to live!" Poor Fool! He has a will to live (at least his mind tells him so). The Fool is alive. He need make no effort to be alive; in fact, he must make effort only if he wishes to cease living. His need to live is irrational. It does not depend on his being *for* life and *against* death, but is a natural result of being born. He has mistaken a natural caution for a rule of life. The second day is called by the Maya, born of air, air being for them the prime element necessary for living. It was also the symbol of higher planes of understanding. This is the most important step the Fool can take, for it places him in a position from whence the TONAL may be observed. He is born of air, has learned to fly above the involvement with the opposites. Life is not the Fool's enemy; life is not out to kill him.

VENUS: This planet rules love and beauty. Its effect is essentially feminine and tends to bring this aspect out in either sex. The Moon and Venus have many compliments, though unlike the Moon, Venus is mostly beneficent and brings happiness and fulfillment. Often brought about by Venus is that state of love which causes those affected to express themselves in music, singing, or writing poetry. Badly aspected, Venus inclines the native to indolence and pleasure seeking and can bestow a superficial attitude towards others and life in general.

VENUS RULES House of Taurus.
DAY: Friday.
PLANTS: Apple, asparagus, beans, birch, deadly nightshade, elderberry, goldenrod, grape, rye, raspberry, strawberry, tansy.
BODY: Kidneys.
METAL: Copper.
FLOWER: Rose.

The Ruler ●●●●

AKBAL ·Born of water ················· 4

DESCRIPTION: A young, virile, spectacularly dressed person is depicted standing erect in front of the dias, on which to his left sits the Consort and to his right, the Priest. He holds in his cupped hands the Maya bar of authority, the MEXQUIMILLI. His helmet is a mask, upon which is a golden cup that spills brilliant green feathers. He wears a 'backpack' of green and rose wings bearing various complex designs. Around his waist is an elaborate belt which, like the Sorcerer's, has two masks hang-

in from it. Behind him hangs a jaguar skin, and behind that and to his left we see the leading edge of the rising sun.

INTERPRETATION: The Ruler is the beginning, the action, the completion, and the reult. Like the Consort in Card 3, he represents creation but by POWER and WILL rather than by feeling and love. The Ruler is the COMPLETED PARENT; he has been balanced. This card is the father/mother and represents self-mastery, realization in action, compassion and stability. It is the card of leadership in all its aspects.

SIGNIFICANCE: The Ruler is the four elements. He is the four seasons; he is North, South, East and West. He is the square of all creation. To achieve his understanding the Ruler had to pass through the four levels of being and unite them in a way that was practical and expedient for the work which he has undertaken to do. To achieve his vision, his past was burned away. To achieve his ability to act, his death had to become his advisor. His emotions are contained in the cup of his heart and do not flow where they will. He is master of his

life and knows nothing about it.

INVERTED: This is the card of the masterful lover, of authority and will, of dominance over and satiation of the sexual partner in any relationship. It is the ultimate expression of masculinity and may seek to dominate younger males sexually. The homoerotic advances of the Ruler do not in any way alter the sexual orientation of the desired person. The sexual actions of the Ruler, regardless of how bizarre, do not have the power to injure or influence the correspondent, except beneficently.

VALUE: Sight.
COLOR: Scarlet **TONE:** C-Natural.
DIRECTION: Northeast.

MEANING: The Fool sees that the Ruler is aware of all aspects of his being at all times. The Ruler is free of his conditioned responses and no longer reacts to the stimulus of the opposites. He is not governed by their pull. There is no division, no unconscious to the Ruler's mind, no hidden part, nothing suppressed. He sees WHAT IS, not what he wants. He holds nothing and so has nothing to lose, has no hopes and so will not be disappointed. The aspect of the Ruler that interests the Fool is the fact that the Ruler acts and does not react. He also is as constructive at every moment as circumstances allow him to be. A reaction is a remembered response, based upon the results of past actions. The Ruler's past is burned away. He has been reborn—that is, born again, not born of woman but born of his own being. It is hard for the Fool to understand all this. The Ruler has integrated within his personality all contradiction. He sees the purpose of fear and does not avoid it, nor does he build it into his psyche in any manner. All fear is the same fear. Fear of being eaten by the jaguar is not internalized as fear of being humiliated. He sees that there is no place within the mind for fear. Fear is a body (gut) response, most appropriate when walking at night in the jungle; but fear of making a mistake of judgment because one will lose face (for rulers do not make mistakes) is an illusion, a non-reality. Most importantly it is a denial of the capacity of the mind to see, understand and make a response that is appropriate and outside his control. Such fear is foolishness, and whatever he may be, the Ruler is no fool. The Fool sees the opposites as destroying each other, as mortal enemies. To the Ruler they are quite different, for he sees the antagonism as complimentary and their colaboration as complete-

ly necessary so that his action will be creative, since creation partakes equally of construction and destruction. He knows that the most enduring action is made up of equal forces, balanced to achieve the required result.

 ARIES: The Ram. The sun is the symbol of the ego and it is enthroned in Aries. Unless afflicted the Arien will be honest in ideals as well as money. Aries natives are thrifty by nature, although in the right mood can be lavish with the things at their disposal. Motivation in business is marked by fairness, and while the Arien never intends to lose by the deal, this attitude denotes a certain blindness which often makes them the victims of exploiters. With so strong an ego involvement, Aries is caught in the rush, in what is comprehended as the headlong movement of the world. Conflict comes from lack of time to think and a carelessness in relating to others.

RULER: Mars.
ENTHRONED: The Sun.
PLANTS: All those that prepare the way on land for other growth. Lichen. Seaweed.
QUALITY: Masculine. Fire.
BODY: Face. Head.
GEM: Amethyst.

The Priest

KAN •Knowledge of evil •••••••••••••••••••••••••••••• 5

INTERPRETATION: The Priest is the informing spirit who initiates the dreamer into the meaning of life and explains its secrets according to the teachings of the ancients. He is the transmitter of tradition and traditional knowledge. The Priest is bound to the society he serves, and is its mentor. He must keep it growing and changing, alive and meaningful.

SIGNIFICANCE: The Priest is the storehouse of the culture. It is he who must stand with one foot in the real world, the world of nature, and the other foot in the artificial world, the world of man-made things, things that cannot exist in nature. He must live in the NOW, and hold on to the PAST. His attribute is hearing, for it is through this sense that words are heard and passed into meaning. The Priest listens to everything and knows what is said. The Priest knows silence and hears confessions.

INVERTED: The priest exhibits a need to conform and places great importance on being socially accepted. He becomes tied to convention and manifests a vested interest in maintaining the status quo. He becomes rigid, tends to exclusion, and deals only with the outer trappings of religion. Superstition takes the place of investigation, and superiority the place of humility and service.

SEXUAL EXPRESSION: The Priest is a woman's masculine aspect, the Animus, the primal image within the feminine subconscious that endows it with rational understanding, a sense of power, and knowledge of its use. This is the card of the celibate, the one who does not suppress sex or fear it, but lets it rest and is not perpetually agitating or stimulating it for gratification and pleasure. It is also the card of the homosexual, latent or overt, male or female. It is the position of the card in relation to other cards that will give it its final reading. Generally it is a passive heterosexual or a homosexual expression card.

VALUE: Hearing. Tradition.
COLOR: Red-Orange. **TONE:** C-Sharp. D-Flat
DIRECTION: Southeast.

MEANING: The Fool finds himself in possession of a great deal of understanding, having

DESCRIPTION: A person startlingly dressed from head to foot in the skin of a jaguar. On his back he wears a 'pack' made of masks and feathers. He holds in his right hand a staff with one living leaf, and to it is tied a gold-colored cloth. In front of him is part of the same jaguar skin that hangs behind the Ruler. He stands on the other end of the dias from the Consort. Around his waist he wears an elaborate belt, with a single mask of the maize god in front. He seems gentle and secure.

a certain clarity about his world and the world of others. What he has not seen is the power that he now has to manipulate and steer others to his desires. He now has clarity and he must overcome it. He sees and he understands and is only too keen to let others know the 'truth.' The Fool cannot hear. Hearing is beyond just listening, and the Fool listens so that he may know when the other has stopped talking, and he may start. Hearing brings one to silence and union with the other. In that silence the Fool may hear the voice of the unknown. The Priest presents the Fool with the principal of a living, mysterious universe. It is symbolized by the staff with the living leaf. The jaguar-dress of the Priest represents the Fire aspect of a person. It is a symbol of the energy and vitality that is available to the Fool and that can be released for his use in the task he has set himself. The Priest is the bridge builder, the PONTIFEX, the one who points the way but does not lead. The Priest is the guru, the teacher, the scientist. He is the investigator and the holder of tradition. It is said that tradition cannot be inherited, it can only be earned with love. He is the holder of the sciences and must teach them as well. The Fool is busy learning to be a saint. He has repressed sex and is determined to be a moral person, so he is in agony. The Priest, as a celibate, is not sexually repressed and certainly makes no effort at moral

practice. The Fool is fixed in his endeavor, is caught in imitation and an endless, useless repetition of dead slogans and mantras. His behavior is eventually more destructive than constructive, which of course was not his intention. On the other hand, the demeanor of the Priest is ultimately more constructive than destructive, although that was NOT his aim. This is because the Priest proceeds from pure activity and adapts himself to circumstances as they present themselves, in a manner that is continually fresh. The Priest does not say "I will be a celibate." He *is* celibate, and this position is not consciously maintained as it is with the Fool. It is the spontaneous outcome of an aware person who does not dream but completes each action in the moment of its being.

 TAURUS: The Bull. The most characteristic feature of Taureans is their gentle, persuasive, and peace-loving dispositions. They are often exploited because of this meekness. They can live amicably with impossible people and rarely lose their temper. Lovers of food and drink, Taureans are self-indulgent. When the Sun is well aspected, it can inhibit the easy flow of Venus energies and bring about a strong, silent, balanced type. Badly aspected, it can cause destructive and hysterical rages, bringing out deep-seated jealousies and angers. As young persons Taureans rarely find worldly success, for their genius tends to flower late, but when it does blossom its nature usually is profound and concentrated.

RULER: Venus—Earth.

EXALTED: Moon.

PLANTS: Mushrooms and fungi that grow near the ground, and those such as truffles that grow under it. Lilies. Spinach.

QUALITY: Feminine. Earth.

BODY: Neck.   Throat.

GEM: Moss Agate.

 # The Lovers

CHACCHAN •Gathering together experience ············· 6

INTERPRETATION: The Lovers present the Fool with the intricacies of relationship and force him to examine love. He must also examine choice, for this is the card of choosing. The man stands under the canopy, protected by the known, by the craft of the Priest. The woman stands under the stars, open to their influence and to the influence of the unknown, however it may manifest itself.

SIGNIFICANCE: The Lovers are caught in the web of image and reality. The Mirror they hold is dark and clouded and affords them no view of each other, yet they point into it. This card indicates a closeness of the ultimate aim of the Fool's journey. It displays a harmony of the inner and outer life. It indicates inspiration and leads to love.

INVERTED: Inspiration fails and the person resorts to choice, trapped in the opposites again. Confusion results in inhibition and vagueness. Quarrels and disharmony result from a need for stability and openness. Things do not flow together, and there is difficulty in completing a work begun.

SEXUAL EXPRESSION: An unadulterated, open, sexual union. This card announces the removal of whatever obstacles were standing in the way of the union. It holds an air of innocence about it, not constrained by establishment morals, for it is a totally moral response to a totally moral act. There is fulfillment on all levels. There is a recognition by each partner of the quality of the other. There is no 'lover' and 'loved one' here, for both are lovers of each other. Peace and harmony reign, and true union is experienced.

VALUE: Sense of smell.
COLOR: Orange. **TONE:** D-Natural.
DIRECTION: East—Above.

MEANING: The Lovers are the last stage of the Fool's progression through the spiritual realm. They present him with a complex array of information, and to comprehend it he must give his UNDIVIDED attention. The Fool's task here is to heal the division within himself. He stands sheltered from the woman within him, from the things he has learned from the Priest within him, from his culture,

DESCRIPTION: Two persons are presented to us on this card. One is a man lightly dressed, standing under a bower similar to the one the Priestess sits under. He holds in his left hand a clouded mirror and points into it with his right hand. The other end of the mirror is held by a woman. She is also lightly dressed and points into the mirror with her left hand. She stands under a starry sky. Growing around her feet are tiny golden flowers. Both figures seem at peace and contented.

by the canopy overhead. He is man, the name giving animal, and by naming he separates, creating an immense unbridgeable chasm between himself and the world of the Nagual. 'I see,' he says, 'I understand, so I will not name.' Poor Fool! That is not the answer. How will you ask your way, when you are lost, if you do not name? The Fool has made a world of things and he is trapped. Caught between the two faces of the world, the Fool is caught in the TONAL, the world of form, the world he has made. He yearns for another world. He searches for the other and tries to name it, and in so doing he destroys it. The mind cannot be used to break the hold of the mind. It is only when there is no distance between himself and the world that the Fool can perceive the world as it is. It is only when he has given up the struggle to see that seeing takes place. The Fool has only one lot of energy available to him; he may use it to struggle or he may use it to see. When seeing takes place, it is the woman speaking. She does not care about the Fool's use of names. She has no need of his labels, for her world takes place in the moment. These are the two worlds within the head of the Fool, the two worlds he must bridge. The brain has two parts. The left hemisphere controls the active hand, contains the intellectualizing centers as well as the speech centers. It could be called the RATIONAL or masculine brain. The right hemisphere is little understood but seems to contain the intuiting faculties. It could be called the INTUITION or the feminine brain. Our society has put great importance on the masculine side and heavily suppressed the feminine side. Not until the Fool has found the balance within himself will it be manifested in the society to which he belongs. A society is a reflection, a conglomerate of all the tiny parts that go to make it up. It has no life of its own. The Fool discovers that he can change, and he can change without choosing. Choice is only possible when there is confusion, when there is involvement with the opposites. When there is seeing there is no choice. When there is seeing there cannot be relationship. Relationship exists between two opposites, the one who gives and the one who takes, the speaker and the listener, the lover and the loved one. With seeing all becomes clear and there is no separation. SEEING IS ACTION WHICH IS LOVE. So the triangle is built at last, the lesson of the Consort has born fruit. The Ruler's name is understood. NEM is the Maya word for ruler. It has two other meanings as well—meditator and mirror. The Ruler, the integrated person, reflects that which is below to that above, and that which is above to that below. The Fool has become a lover of himself. He stands in awe and wonder before the extraordinary creature he is, but he must not indulge himself, for the journey has just begun.

GEMINI: The Twins. The strength of Gemini is in brain and nerve, not heart. Geminis have fine minds, good memories, and are capable of accurate knowledge. As a general rule they are receptive and intuitive. Natives of this sign can display much force and a great variety of talent. Gemini is the most versatile sign of the Zodiac, and those born under the sign are of a restless nature, very logical and adept at argument. They make excellent managers, love to travel, and are not particularly concerned with body comforts. On the other hand a badly aspected Gemini can be superficial and shallow. They have a tendency to see both sides of a problem and can therefore show indecisiveness, with resultant dissatisfaction and frustration. Gemini may manifest a state of continual discontent and rancor.

RULER: Mercury.
PLANTS: Mosses, bromiliads, all epiphytes (air-growing and hanging plants). Madder. Tansy.
QUALITY: Masculine—Air.
BODY: Shoulders, collar-bone, lungs, arms.
GEM: Beryl. Pearl.

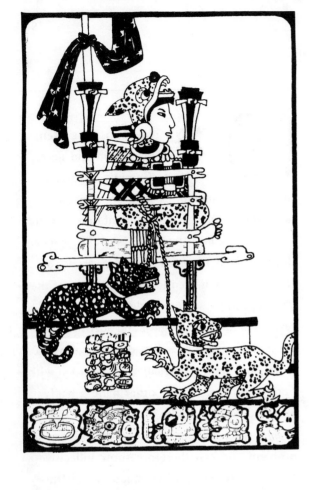

The Warrior

CIMI   •One dies ·· 7

DESCRIPTION: A young man is pictured sitting in a square litter, or carrying chair. He is dressed as a jaguar Knight. Attached to the chair is a starry banner that projects up into the Priestess card; also tied to the chair are two jaguars, one black and one white. Although the cats appear subdued and tame, they are still savage. The Knight is seated on a dias which has an inscription upon it.

INTERPRETATION: This is the first card of the mental realm and the Warrior seems self-contained, poised, ready for whatever may come. The Warrior is in a state of 'choiceless awareness.' The jaguars seem to be a personification of the black and white columns in the Priestess card.

SIGNIFICANCE: Triumph over besetting problems. Victory in matters of money or ill health. This is the card of ability and a responsible attitude towards all aspects of one's life. The Warrior is serious toward whatever task he may take on, or that takes him on.

INVERTED: The card still represents a triumph, but an amoral one, or even downright deceit leading to victory. An unbalanced life or uncontrolled passion. A self-indulgent attitude that leads to downfall.

SEXUAL EXPRESSION: The Warrior is not only the conqueror of women but also very skilled in overcoming whatever barriers may stand between him and the woman he desires. The Warrior is equally skilled at extricating himself from any relationship without ill feelings from the partner. A reversed card does not alter the Warrior's attitudes but leaves his paramour devastated and in anguish over the union, principally because she does not want to let go of the relationship.

VALUE: Speech.
COLOR: Orange-Yellow.
TONE: D-Sharp. E-Flat.
DIRECTION: East-Below.

MEANING: In the Lovers card the Fool dealt with choice. Here in the mental realm he will begin to see the ramifications of his choices. He will also become aware of the manner in which his choices come about. The Warrior is a person completely at one with the environment in which he is sustained, agile and unencumbered by sentiment or "personal history." The Warrior knows that each act that is undertaken may be his last act. He is alone. Death is the very root of his life, and in this knowledge it is not possible for him to do other than perform impeccably. The Warrior's way of living is not one of introspection or mystical transcendence, but one of presence in the world in which he finds himself. Having his anchor in complete knowledge of the fact of imminent death, the Warrior is free from having to speculate about living. This places him in the position of a juggler who must balance the terror and wonder of being born into a world that is, in essence, incomprehensible.

The Warrior deals with speech and all of its implications. His first battle is with the chatter that goes on in the head and it is this battle that sets the Warrior on his path. He is concerned with seeing his own fear, overcoming anxiety and bad eating habits, and stopping the internal chatter. The Warrior is concerned with total revolution, total being made anew, not exchange. The Warrior card is also the card of health, for a Warrior can only bring off the revolution if he is in top physical condition and the revolution begins in his own body. The Warrior's body must be tuned to the world, if he is to influence a change in that world.

The Fool has always thought he was changing, but now he sees that all he ever did was to exchange one thing for another, one problem for another. He never really was able to be totally new, totally different. The Fool cultivated a vocabulary believing it would help him analyze his world, and that turned out to be so.

In fact, it did more. By using words to understand the world, he created that world, limited it and defined it. Words and the faculty of speech can never free him from the world. To be free of the world the Warrior must be in it totally, not divided, not concerned, not worried about it. Only that complete commitment to it can give freedom from it. The opposites are active and savage but harnessed by the total attention of the Warrior.

CANCER: The Crab. Cancer is a nurturing sign representing the mother principle. It is a sign whose energy is directed toward home and family. Natives of the sign usually have a strong imagination and tend to be very sensitive. Cancer people tend to be good business persons, excellent at amassing and controlling money. The image-making faculty is also very strong, and when this is the case they make excellent actors, writers, and poets. A particularly good occupation for a Cancer native is that of journalist, especially those who specialize in writing a column, since Cancerians are not the best at objective reporting. When the sign is badly aspected, the native tends more towards a life of fantasy and a feeling of deep-rooted inner insufficiency, which is often offset by the playing of roles to gain sympathy and respect.

RULER: The Moon.
PLANTS: Beans, bananas, cabbage, lettuce and most leafy vegetables, ferns, lotus, melons, mushrooms, pumpkin, sugarcane, watercress, willow, and violets.
QUALITY: Feminine—Water.
BODY: The chest and stomach.
GEM: Emerald.

The Cactus

MAN-IK   •Overcomes death ···························· 8

INTERPRETATION: There is the ability to bring one's nature into harmony. Fear must be understood, for it is at the root of any search for security. There is no place in the mind for fear of any kind. With the understanding of fear, material desires assume a reasonable place in the life of the enquirer and do not over-whelm it with greed. Fears are released.

SIGNIFICANCE: The Cactus stands for en-durance, the passive strength that enables one to see an action through to its completion. The Cactus is not free, for it grows in a pot, yet it has reached maturity, is in flower, and will complete its natural cycle regardless of its "imprisonment."

INVERTED: The surety of endurance has crumbled and the fear of failure has taken over. The soil in the pot has turned sour. The nerve fails the Fool and defeat and surrender are inevitable.

SEXUAL EXPRESSION: This is the card of the PASSIVE DOMINANT, the person who gets their desires fulfilled by being there, unmovable. It also resresents the fantasy aspects of sex, the activity of the mind as it uses the body to gratify what it believes to be its needs. Inverted, it becomes the card of onanism, masturbation. Sex is initiated by the mind and fantasy plays a strong part in it.

VALUE: Taste. Endurance.
COLOR: Yellow.
TONE: E-Natural.
DIRECTION: North-Above.

MEANING: Through work the Fool has at-tained a "seeing," which frees him from the constant whimsical changes of mood and desire that previously controlled him. He now "controls" them. The control the Fool exer-cises is passive, for the "dying" he learned as a Warrior has now become "habit," a part of his autonomic system. There is no longer the need for effort; he thinks about it no longer; he has overcome. The Fool discovers the passive inner strength of steadfast purpose, as contrasted with the positive outer strength of action. There is virtue in the Fool's life, and this inner strength makes its presence felt. This passive

DESCRIPTION: A large green cactus of the San Pedro type grows in a fancy pot that is white with black decorations. The decoration shows a temple and two priests. The Cactus is in full blossom and sitting in its branches is a small white bird. On the right bottom corner there is the smoke from the basin in the Sage card, and above that a small part of the lintel over the temple door. At the bottom are glyphs on the temple platform.

strength makes the order in his life, for this strength accepts both nothing and everything. All is considered and allowed to find its own level by its own weight.

Many of the American deserts were once fresh-water lakes, surrounded by lush water plants. As the climate changed and became hotter, the lakes dried up. Most of the plants were not able to adjust and so they perished. Cacti have descended from these water plants and by admirable adaptation and mutation were able to survive the change, adapting to the new environments.   The Cactus belongs to that part of the vegetable kingdom which provides mankind with intoxicants and hallucinogens. The Cactus is native to the Americas and has been introduced into all other countries as an exotic. A great many indigenous religions have taken advantage of its strange properties to aid them in their search for God.

The Maya name for this day is MAN-IK, that is, one overcomes death. Endurance requires an attitude not unlike death. The quality it exhibits is only understood when it has been overcome. This fortitude, this endurance, is what gives the Fool the ability to pass through trials and overcome them.

<u>LEO</u>: No matter how humble the origins of a Leo, they take it for an obvious fact that in one manner or another, they are superior. They are born monarchs. The Leo native is big-hearted, liberal (to a point), honorable, and lordly. They would never take advantage of a rival's weakness to achieve their ideals. The first consideration of a Leo, however, is self and self-achievement. Leos are lovers of status, feeling themselves to be always somewhere near the top. It is said that they love occupations that are dangerous, sometimes dealing with fire and explosives. Many Leo natives are concerned wth the production of nuclear fission. In business they tend to be managers and directors. There is also a love of ornamentation and the display of luxury. Badly aspected, they can be vicious and unthinking in the speed with which they strike out against an enemy. Usually a Leo will not let up an attack until the foe is completelydemolished. Pride and vanity can be the undoing of a Leo.

<u>RULER</u>: Sun.
<u>EXAULTED</u>: Neptune.
<u>PLANTS</u>: Pines and firs, all plants that have cones, and cobs such as maize.
<u>QUALITY</u>: Masculine—Fire.
<u>BODY</u>: Sides, back, heart and spinal column.
<u>GEM</u>: Ruby.

The Sage

LAMAT •Overcomes material ······················ 9

DESCRIPTION: A man kneels in the center of the picture, pointing upward at a lintel over the temple door that depicts two men in a canoe. They are going in different directions and between them is the eye of the sun, decorated with water lily buds. With his other hand the kneeling man points down at a basin in which a fire blazes and from which much smoke pours out. Behind the Sage is the starry sky, in which is cut a small square passage with a light at its end. Lining up with the spine of the sage is a staff with one living leaf on it.

INTERPRETATION: The Sage is alone so that he may hear the inner voice speak. There is a need for quiet so that the path may be seen clearly. The lintel demonstrates the confusion that was the life of the Sage, for it shows two men in a boat and they are going in different directions. The tunnel in the sky is the openness the Sage requires to "see" the way out.

SIGNIFICANCE: The Sage has no needs, for the universe provides everything that is necessary to sustain him. He makes no demands whatsoever. He makes no effort either, yet he survives. The mystery of existence (staff) supports him. The fire in the bowl warms him. On the bowl are depicted the opposites (awake and asleep), and the fire makes a triangle of conciliation between them.

INVERTED: There is a reluctance to give up a cause that is lost, a refusal to heed a wise voice. The person is not trusting of their own quiet voice inside.

SEXUAL EXPRESSION: There is mastery of sex. It no longer claims the attention all of the time. There is an ease and grace about the act, for nothing is expected of it other than what it gives. There is sexual enjoyment of the highest order. The Sage does not choose his partners; when it is right, they are there, for he has the understanding and wisdom to be able to satisfy.

VALUE: Touch.
COLOR: Yellow-Green.
TONE: F-Natural.
DIRECTION: North—Below.

MEANING: The Sage has no needs, since the universe provides everything needed. The Sage shows the Fool that there is such a thing as freedom. He demonstrates that freedom is freedom from all things, else it cannot exist. Freedom is not, as the Fool believes, freedom from fear, from financial oppression, from sickness, age, or death. Being rich does not free one from poverty; poverty is a state of mind, a conditioned response. Freedom is not a conditioned response and cannot have a cause—one is free or one is not. It is another of those things that does not admit to degrees. It is or it is not. Mostly it is not. All search takes place within the known; therefore, the object of the search is already within the field of experience or of idea. The Fool has an idea of what freedom is, then searches to find that ideal. How can that be freedom?

Wisdom is when freedom is, for freedom is its own reward and cannot be learned. It is discovered in the "seeing" clearly, which is the way of the Warrior. Freedom is the fortitude of the Cactus, which enables it to pluck from the world around it whatever it needs to survive.

LAMAT is the name of this stage in the Fool's journey. It is the struggle to overcome the material, the struggle to overcome the struggle itself. Behind the Sage is the vast expanse of the starry sky—his consciousness with its bright and hidden parts. This is the world which the Sage must explore over and over again, seeing but not naming, trying to not try, working to not work. The Fool is a lost traveller on a lost planet in an undiscovered galaxy. His question is "If I don't know where I am, and don't care where I am, can I be said to be lost?"

VIRGO: The Virgan seems on the surface hardly to have the talent for practical organizational ability, yet the natives of this sign do. They have a capacity for analytical thought, as well as the ability to interpret accurately all the conflicting information gathered by the senses. As a rule Virgo natives are conscientious in their dealings with others and tend to exhibit very high principles. They are excellent learners and are often mechanically dexterous, very good in occupations which use the fingers or the toes— typing, dancing, drafting, craftsmanship, etc. Badly aspected, Virgans tend to worry excessively, become highly nervous, and tend to vacillate between periods of socializing (which they tend to do badly) and periods of solitude. There is a tendency to do things in excess in either direction. There are more spinsters and bachelors in this sign than in any other.

RULER: Mercury.
MUTABLE: Earth.
PLANTS: Cereals, wheat, oats, barley, grasses and sedges.
QUALITY: Feminine—Earth.
BODY: Intestines, digestive tract.
GEM: Jasper.

The Wheel

MULUC • Reaping rewards of effort •••••••••••••••••••• 10

INTERPRETATION: The wheel is a mandala, a symbol of psychic wholeness, and as such alludes to the laws which govern the whole of existence. It embodies the principle of rhythmic change, within which nothing is constant.

SIGNIFICANCE: Round and round the wheel goes and where it stops no one knows. Absolute chance brings success to the Fool Good fortune arrives against all hope. The laws of chance bestow their favor.

INVERTED: Chance avoids the Fool; Lady Luck looks the other way. This is the downward trend, the time when one must wait for the odds to turn up in one's favor. They will . . . eventually.

SEXUAL EXPRESSION: The ups and downs of sexual passions within the individual, the menstruation cycle within women, all of the cyclical events relating to a person's sexual life are dealt with in this card. The individual changes, is never constant. Reversed, the meaning does not change, except that it is the down-

ward trend in a cycle, before it starts the upward swing.

VALUE: Wealth—poverty. Learning.
COLOR: Violet.
TONE: B-Flat. A-Sharp.
DIRECTION: West.

MEANING: In the great silent pool of NOW the wheel turns. Life and death, being and nonbeing, it turns as one TONAL succeeds another, one age after another, movement and memory. The lesson taught the Fool in front of the great calendar stone is that movement is born within the conflict between opposite polarities. Movement is time, speed is time, and the Fool understands that time and its passage is but movement and memory.

The wheel is held in place by two stones. They demonstrate that in the end even time is bound and finite. Between the two extremes of time past and future time is the great treasure, the great reward, the living Now. On the wheel the only freedom is to enjoy its laws and motion, to live in harmony with these laws. The reward

DESCRIPTION: Around the outside edge of a large wheel are Maya glyphs, as yet indecipherable. Inside the rim is depicted a snake swallowing its tail. Inside of that is a rubbing taken from the Aztec callendar stone. It is composed of a circle on which the twenty day symbols are drawn and a cross with a human face at its center. The wheel is surmounted by a parrot and anchored between two stones. Below the wheel is pictured a jaguar nurturing its cub.

of a successful journey is a new age.

There is nothing the Fool can do to bring about the change he so desires. When he acts he merely substitutes one thing for another. To escape into Jesus, or Buddha, or the Tree of Life, or alcohol is still only to escape; no real change has taken place. Only the fullness of life will select the moment when the lightning will strike. Fortune smiles, and the joke is always YOU poor Fool.

MULAC, reaping the reward of effort, is the Maya name for this step on the journey. Plant the seed and eventually the harvest will come around. Once the law is understood, one may participate in the rhythm one may take part in the dance, and have the power to break the circle, to distort that rhythm and to trip the dancers. Around and around the wheel goes, and where it stops no one knows.

4 JUPITER: This planet rules fortune and fate. Its effect is beneficent, and it adds gloss and quality to whatever it influences. Jupiter is wholesome and represents nothing but the best, yet it symbolizes the culture of man and all its implications of good and evil. This is the planet of money, and those who have it well aspected never need for cash. Jupiter rules the Supreme Court and many of the judicial branches of government. In a class society, he represents the upper class, the nobility. Badly aspected, Jupiter is responsible for class and racial bigotry. Poor judicial practice also is a result of its bad side, as is snobbery and all forms of class distinction.

JUPITER RULES: House of Sagittarius.
DAY: Thursday.
PLANTS: Anice, apricot, acorn, beech-nut, cinnamon, chicory, clove, figs, grapes, myrrh, mulberry, marjoram, nutmeg, oak, olives, tomatoes.
METAL: Tin.
FLOWER: Dahlia.

The Balance

OC

•Enters fully into matter ············· 11

INTERPRETATION: The sword cuts at preconceptions and prejudices of all kinds in the hope of striking a balance. Only a well-balanced mind that is clearly objective can decide, for decision is division, and the cutting of one movement begins another.

SIGNIFICANCE: The balance is directly connected to the flow of energy, and the tip of the scale indicates the direction of this flow. The Wheel showed us something of the operation of chance in culture. Here the Fool learns that all culture is decision. This is the card of the handling of energy. It is the world brought about by the Fool's decisions in life, his likes and dislikes.

INVERTED: The mind is biased and full of preconceived notions. There is no "seeing" of the effects of decision-making. Because no decisions are taken, they are only reactions, and there will be no decision until it is forced.

SEXUAL EXPRESSION: In this card you get just what is coming to you. There is a strong pull in the direction of sex, a pull that is not emotionally colored but rather is balanced and stable. This is the card of sexual cause and effect. Rewards are earned and punishments are received. Badly aspected, sex is the undoing of the questioner. Willfulness and lack of integrity are manifest. The mind convinces an unwilling partner with emotional blackmail.

VALUE: Work—Decisions.
COLOR: Green
TONE: F-Sharp. G-Flat.
DIRECTION: Northwest.

MEANING: This is the last card of the mental realm, the realm of thought. If the Fool is to make any decision, he must enter fully into it, with no half-heartedness. The Fool finds himself in the position of a judge, operating a balance with only one side, for he must define need, not equality. He must separate dream from reality, fantasy from fact. This is where the Fool makes his world, a product of all the decisions he has ever made. He decides it and defines it by disposing of the energy available within a given situation.

DESCRIPTION: A finely dressed man stands on a step and holds in his right hand a sword, from which comes lightning that divides into two streams. One stream strikes a skull at the base of the balance; the other stream continues on down and passes beyond the bottom of the picture. Over the man's left arm is an oblong shield, or perhaps it is a folded cloak.

To decide is to divide. All decision destroys innocence. It is the active principle entered into by the Lovers when they assumed authority for their world. Creation and destruction are the two sides of the judge's sword; he cannot use one side without using the other as well. To decide is to choose and the Fool is enmeshed in comparison. To make a decision the Fool cannot compare. He must see each decision as unique, carrying its own pattern of division. When the Fool is handed a cake, he decides which piece he wants, takes it, and from that moment on he has no interest in the rest of the cake—he has in effect released it. The sword of decision has a side called division and a side called release.

There is no decision that does not carry with it a sense of loss; and so the skull sits at the base of the balance and the lightning strikes it, for the restriction of energy inevitably results in a loss of some energy, since the act itself requires energy as well. Energy is used to block off energy and move it in the direction required by the divider. The Fool at the balance is both the user and the victim of the use to which he puts the energy. Only his total immersion in the energy of the decision can free him from loss and corruption of his act.

LIBRA: The Balance. These are the best mannered of all of the signs of the Zodiac. A Libran speaks quietly and slowly. They tend towards being well-dressed beautiful people, very conscious of their bodies. The Libran has a strong tendency towards self-love. This is not the most intellectual sign but does show a natural slyness and a great talent for self-preservation. The Libra native is an excellent promoter and does very well acting as an agent for others. Libran energy enhances all relationships, being more objective about them and allowing time to foster cooperation instead of competition. These natives are fine at arranging functions and gatherings when the arts and cultural programs are favored. Libra is the time to make and negotiate contracts, and a Libran is most apt at drawing up the type of contract in which all parties may benefit and feel contented about the deal.

RULER: Venus.
PLANTS: Iris, lily, orchid, plants that exhibit an exact symmetry in their outer structure (such as the Stapelia family).
QUALITY: Masculine—Air.
BODY: Kidneys.
GEM: Diamond.

Hanged Man

CHUEN   Burning without flame ·····················12

DESCRIPTION: A person hangs upside down with the left leg and arm tied to a gibbet (a hangman's tree), and the right leg and arm tied to a living tree that is in blossom. A radiation comes from the body and the blue sky is overcast with storm clouds turning an ominous red. The gibbet and the living tree are rising from a fertile green plain.

INTERPRETATION: All dependence on mind is brought to a standstill; no movement is possible. There can now be a complete reversal of one's usual way of seeing things. When the mind surrenders, the voice of prophesy speaks.

SIGNIFICANCE: This is the first card of the emotional realm and its shows that the Fool's values are now turned topsy turvy. The mind has been brought to a total impasse and is at the end of its teather. The mind's limits will be exposed by the emotions, which will prod and test those limits until all suffering is laid bare.

INVERTED: A resistance makes life impossible. No grounds for negotiation. The Hanged Man must find his own way off the tree. His emotional life is his own hands. Stagnation of emotional response.

SEXUAL EXPRESSION: There is too much discernment in sexual matters. The person becomes hung up between the sexual ideal and the reality of sexual needs, often 'solving' the problem by suspending the sexual inclinations and becoming asexual.

VALUE: Mind.
COLOR: Pale Blue.
TONE: G-Sharp. A-Flat.
DIRECTION: Center. East to West.

MEANING: The mind has come to a standstill, a total impasse. This is a holy position, and holy means whole or complete, implying total surrender. TOTAL surrender, WHOLE surrender—there can be no synthetic surrender here. This totality of action is the sacrifice necessary for the Fool to comprehend the "cosmic order."

The Hanged Man is the absolute paradox, the burning without flame, CHUEN, the losing of the self in order to find the self. For the Fool's edification we have here a graphic depiction of the illusion of "I," hung between the dead past and the living, blossoming now. The I is born when it believes it has a self, separate from the body. Having separated itself by its view of things, it finds itself in what it believes (not without reason) to be a hostile world. The I never perceives of itself as hostile, but as defensive, defending its right to be left alone. The Fool is confused. LIFE, existence, is a whole (holy) thing, a complete thing, yet he feels himself to be a separate entity. How can this be? If he is separate, the whole cannot include him and therefore is not whole. Once more the paradox: he who loses himself shall also find himself. When the "I" is forgotten, wholeness is once more.

The Fool must be consumed inwardly by his suffering, the paradox comes when one is caught in the neutral ground between the opposites. This is actually the opportunity of the Fool's lifetime. At last, stuck at the center, he has the possibility of surrender—will he make use of it?

NEPTUNE: This planet rules the subconscious, the repository of secret and illusory things. Neptune moves through the Zodiac very slowly, which accounts for its ponderous and secretive nature. It is most influenced by the sign it is in, since it stays there so long. Neptune people are attracted to the flashy and dramatic, and strongly attracted to the occult and the mystery of the unknown. Neptunians love sensation and so are drawn to music, art, and poetry. The Cinema is their pre-eminent field. Being natural prevaricators, they make good light actors, excellent comics, and flashy soloists. Badly aspected, a native may live in a world that borders on the unacceptable to others. There is a tendency to think that others are plotting one's downfall.

NEPTUNE RULES: House of Pisces.
DAY: Afternoon.
PLANTS: Asparagus, borage, chervil, cocoa, chestnut, ginseng, leeks, lichen, mint, and turnip.
METAL: Neptunium.
FLOWER: Arctotis.

Death Man

E B · Begins the climb out ·················· 13

DESCRIPTION: This is a startling card painted in bright colors. A skeletal figure stomps across a green and fertile landscape. Behind the figure of Death are brilliant fiery clouds, and behind those clouds seems to be the light of a new day dawning. The figure holds a shield and two darts in one hand, while the other is limp and empty. There are flowers growing up between skulls.

THIS IS NOT A CARD OF PHYSICAL DEATH.

INTERPRETATION: This is a card of renewal and transformation, a card of the dying-to-emotions that hold one back and does not allow for growth and new ideas. It is the act of dying to the past, to habit, and the old personality. The death of the past allows freedom to be born.

SIGNIFICANCE: To the person involved in the mystery of existence, life is an eternal daydream to which death can put no end, for death cannot properly exist in the world of thinking. Death is an action, not an idea, it is seen as a passing to another state. Death is not an end in itself, it is not separate from life but is a part of one's life.

INVERTED: It points to disaster, likely on a social level: political trouble, revolution, upheaval in government which could mean a boss, even a dominant partner, one who is in authority. There could be a temporary stagnation in the realm of ideas, a condition where prejudice is considered an original thought.

SEXUAL EXPRESSION: This card signals a great change in one's sexual life. This can be good or bad. If one is lonely and frustrated sexually, that may change; if one is contented and happy in one's sexual arrangements, that may change. All of the change is necessary for growth, although the change may be considered undesirable at the time.

VALUE: Motion, change. Ally.
COLOR: Greenish- blue.
TONE: G-Natural.
DIRECTION: Southwest.

MEANING: Death stands on the bones and skulls of those who ventured on the path, didn't have the stamina for the task, and tried to withdraw. For the Fool there can be no going back. He understands there is no "back" to which he may return. All roads lead to where the Fool stands.

The Fool's death is his friend, his ally and helper. Death gives a perspective to the Fool's lie and becomes a remarkable measuring stick by which to consider his actions and gauge their importance. With death as a friend, it is difficult to threaten the Fool, very hard to persuade him into a course of action that is superficial or dangerous.

The Dead Man striding across the plains of the emotions is the great equalizer, cutting down everything that crosses the path. The name of Death has been heard over and over again by the Fool. Now here it is, DEATH, face to face, the ultimate terror of the mind, the eternal, one, true friend, the way out of the trap of paradox. Death breaks the hold of the mind and is the one action the mind cannot cope with. The mind may lie, cheat, evade, but do what it will, it must some time face what it sees as its nemisis.

The Mayas titled this day in the journey EB, that is, the climb out. The implication is that one has reached the bottom, the foundation upon which the mind has built its "palace of illusions,"and there is only one direction now, and that is up. The Fool begins the climb out of illusion.

SCORPIO: The Scorpion. The Scorpio native is magnetic, charismatic, passionate, but, also detached from the everyday superficial aspects of things. Scorpio wishes to experience the entire spectrum of human activity. A Scorpio is crafty and cunning, understanding the weaknesses and strengths of others and not afraid of using what is known about others to gain an objective. Scorpios are excellent at ferreting out information from others. This is a sign of extremes that can express itself as cultured and polished or crude and vulgar, as best suits the purpose. Scorpios make excellent singers and orators. Badly aspected, it makes for pugnatious people who love to fight over anything at all. When quarrelsome they are not respectors of "fairness," and dirty tricks is the preferred way of in-fighting.

RULER: Mars. Pluto.
PLANTS: Aroids (arum family) and palms, all plants with a phallic signature.
QUALITY: Feminine—Water.
BODY: Sex organs.
GEM: Spanish Topaz.

Temperate Man

BEN • Growing on through 14

INTERPRETATION: The tempering of the opposites so that they may be brought together in an enduring form. Working in harmony with others to bring about modifications in things and result in good management. This is the card of the chemist or alchemist, the pharmacist, the dispenser of drugs for healing.

SIGNIFICANCE: The temperate person knows what they do. When they eat, they eat; when they drink, they drink. They know a thought as a thought and nothing more. There is an understanding of the order of things because there is no separation from them. There is no possibility of giving "space" to another, only the possibility of defining one's own space.

INVERTED: The combination of events is unfortunate, any mixture is explosive, not amenable to any combination. Partnerships break up because of competing interests and conflicts in personal affairs. Poor judgment is indicated.

SEXUAL EXPRESSION: There can not be any impetuous action leading to sexual gratifica-

tion. There can only be an exact return, penny for penny so to speak, of the original investment. There is a unique harmony of the biological needs and emotional desires that is enjoyed through temperance of the sexual urge and discipline of the appetites.

VALUE: Adaptation. Vibration.
COLOR: Blue.
TONE: G-Sharp. A-Flat.
DIRECTION: West above.

MEANING: This is the Fool's place of predeliction, his place for meeting with powers. It is the place on the emotional plane which faces the setting sun, the place where secrets are revealed. Here every rock, every pebble, every blade of grass, and every thought is under the care of the Fool. He is responsible for this place, because the powers demand it. Every worm that lives here is his friend; he can use them and they can use him. The sacrifice of the Hanged Man card made this place of refuge possible. It is the result of the Fool's ability to understand the cosmic order and the relationship he, of necessity, has with it. The

DESCRIPTION: This is a beautiful card, all pink and blue. The sun is in mid-heaven and a rainbow sheds its light on the scene. A figure is in the center of the card. He wears a simple white kilt and carries a staff wit its living leaf. The young man pours water upon the ground, starry water, a great deal more water than the jug could ever hold. There is peace and balance in the card.

sacrifice involved all of those things the Fool was capable of doing and all that he may be able to develop (but because of wisdom does not develop). He sees the destruction of the ecology that would result from upsetting of the balance of things. He respects the balance upon which the natural world has its anchor.

BEN, meaning growing on through, is the name given by the Mayas to this stage. The old tarot gave it the attribute of vibration. The Latin root of vibration is *vibrere,* which means to oscillate in harmony. From this root also come the words *vita,* meaning life, *viva,* meaning to live, and the English word "viper," a snake. The origin of the word is still the same, *vibora*; that which vibrates. The way out, begun in the Death card, is continued in the Temperance card. The Seed has sprouted and its pale green shoots have broken through the earth into the air and the light of the sun.

The Fool has the power to create a temperate society, a place where there is something of everything but not too much of anything. The Fool knows that this place must first exist within himself. He knows that it is a place of harmony and balance where he may rest for a while on his journey up, a place where he has his skin sensitized to the vibration of the universe.

SAGITTARIUS: The Archer. Sagittarians always exhibit a fine sense of humor, the result of an object awareness of the things around them. These natives have a strong desire for respectability and a fear of public opinion. Sagittarians are often attracted to the law and make fine attorneys, for they love to reward the righteous and punish the wicked. Sagittarians work hard to advance their mates in social positions and are proud of their station in life and their home, which will always reflect this status. The natives of this sign love the outdoors, taking great pleasure in communing with nature. Sagittarians are excellent at weeding the garden of their natures, experiencing no difficulty in removing old and outworn ideas from their philosophy of life. They make good religious leaders, being both cultured and refined. Adversely aspected, there is a tendency to be mealy-mouthed. Sagittarians can be incredible nags, driving their companions to the brink of madness by their ability to not let up. They can be very pompous.

RULER: Jupiter.
PLANTS: Sagittarius rules the great forests, all large trees, and trees bearing catkins, such as beach and elm.
QUALITY: Masculine. Fire.
BODY: Thighs and hips.
GEM: Red Garnet.

 # Bound Man

INTERPRETATION: There is no devil except of our own creation. There is no bondage except of our own doing. In this card the temptation is to disregard human dignity in favor of profit. It represents the short-term profit, which is the inevitable long-term loss. Sickness is indicated by the position of this card in a spread.

SIGNIFICANCE: The serpent of time, continuance, is over the head of the woman (right brain). The torch in the position of extinction is over the man's head (left brain). The two skulls on the head of Xipe-Totec are the door into matter (birth) and the door out of matter (death). The two people struggle with their bonds, but the harder they struggle the tighter the bonds become. There are two symbols of understanding in this card, the mask and the tail of the serpent, but neither person is aware of them, so the way out cannot be used at all.

INVERTED: Bondage to a material existence is overcome; the way out is seen and used. Pride is overcome. There is genuine understanding and a good laugh is the result. Laughter clears the soul and the mind.

SEXUAL EXPRESSION: This is the card of insatiable sexual appetite, the disturbed person to whom sex is the only communication availabe. It represents the extremes of all sexual abuse that can be practiced.

VALUE: Laughter.
COLOR: Indigo (blue-violet).
TONE: A-Natural.
DIRECTION: West below.

MEANING: The Fool is held by his every idea, every thought, every feeling, he is bound by his flesh and his appetites. Reason is the Fool's bondage. What place has reason in the emotions of the Fool? Reason is a laughable view of the TONAL, since by its very reasonableness, it exposes itself as a lie. The Bound Man indicates that this card is where all dark passions lurk within each breast, it represents a person's talent for evil and blindness.

This is a dangerous encounter for the Fool, for here he meets directly with the energy of the

DESCRIPTION: A man and a woman stand back to back, lightly bound to a large mask in th center of the card. The mask is that of Xipe-Totec, the god of spring. He holds in his left hand, over the head of the man, a torch that he is in the act of extinguishing. Over the woman's head he holds a serpent. Between the man and the woman is the tail of the Feathered Serpent, which is out of the card below.

inner self. He must do battle once more, and if he loses the "ego" will reassert itself stronger than ever. The "I" exerts itself by convincing the Fool that he has won the battle. The "I" will then display all of the signs of the vanquished and convince the Fool that he is a realized being. If the challenge of the collective unconscious can be met, recognized, and brought within the light of the conscious, then the forces of darkness are transformed into the powers of light, there is no unconscious, except that the "I" makes it so, for the unconscious is made of all those encounters which seem to threaten the "I." Consciousness is a whole, which is known to the Fool all of the time. It's just that he pretends certain painful things are not there at all.

Fool, wash yourself entirely clean (IX) of your bondage, and laugh at yourself, for after all you are the butt of the joke! Laugh yourself clean.

CAPRICORN: The Goat. The natives of this sign are without vanity, unsure of themselves on many levels yet possessed of a quiet warmth. Probably the most ambitious of all signs, Capricorn prefers to work behind the scenes, for fundamentally they are doubters and pessimists. Most Capricorn natives have a bad childhood, and the scars of these experiences tend to carry over throughout life. Capricorn energies tend toward the practical and the concrete, for they are security oriented. More than any other sign, Capricorn is attracted to the weird, uncanny, mysterious, and the bizarre. These natives are obsessed with money and economy, an aspect that can make its mark in every corner of their lives. When badly aspected it can become a chronic meanness, not only regarding money but every aspect of the personality. Because of this relationship with thrift, they make excellent self-employed persons. They have a discipline which enables them to overcome obstacles that would swamp less controlled persons.

RULER: Saturn.
PLANTS: All plants having separate petals to their flowers.
QUALITY: Feminine. Earth.
BODY: Knees.
GEM: Onyx. Sardonyz.

Released Man

INTERPRETATION: A change will upset old ideas and bring a chance for realization. A new way of seeing one's life is possible, and the ambition that drove one on will now be played out by a change in circumstances.

SIGNIFICANCE: One divides to secure a piece of the pie—having the piece one wants, one releases the other piece. The Divided Man is a mirror image of the Hanged Man, who was tied to the past and the now. Here the now (lightning) casts the two out of the past (the knowledge structure of the temple). The two people are the left and right hemispheres of the brain. Recognizing the division to be what it is, one is released from any expectations. One is cast into freedom; one does not choose it. One *can't* choose it. One merely *wants* it, and that won't set one free.

INVERTED: There is very little change, for this is a card of things being turned upside down, and upside down is up side down. The implication is that the cost and the struggle is great.

SEXUAL EXPRESSION: The sexual personalty is turned on its head. There can be a stopping of sexual activity. Sexual abuses will be brought to an end, with peace discovered in the beauty of celibacy. New understanding of the sexual attitude is discovered and herd instincts about sex are no more.

VALUE: Grace. Release.
COLOR: Scarlet.
TONE: C-Natural.
DIRECTION: North.

MEANING: All of the Fool's attachments, all the things he holds to, the beliefs and reasonings that are so "logical," are struck by the lightning of release and burned to the ground. The temple is the "I," for on the roof comb are depicted three eyes. The middle one is single and ornate, and behind it are two others, the eyes of the silent watcher, the quiet, still, seeing that knows what to do. There are twenty-two steps up to the temple, which represent the twenty-two cards of the higher arcana. All that one "knows" must be struck by the lightning and burned to the ground. All

DESCRIPTION: The center of the card is a temple tower with a straw roof and an elaborate comb. The temple is at the top of the tower and 22 steps must be climbed to reach it. The lightning from the sword of decision strikes the tower and sets it ablaze. Two individuals are thrown head first from the temple. Flames and cinders are beginning to fill the air.

of the systems of knowledge that have supported the Fool must go, even that system which has taken him this far. All dependency must go. The process by which the Fool binds knowledge to himself is selective. He is the decider, and the divider, and it is inevitable that this house of knowledge, built on sand will fall. That which happens has its own reasons and rarely ever matches the pictures that the mind makes of the event. The logic of events does not correspond to the logic of the mind.

Understanding cannot be developed. It is not a process that takes place in time, not an accumulative process. It cannot be learned, it can only be invited, and it happens in the moment. Understanding is the lightning bolt that strikes the tower of knowledge and sets it aflame. It is the lightning of understanding that lights the candle of freedom, that illumines the darkness of the Fool's reason.

MEN—perfection is close, for here the Fool is caught in the tide and swell of the emotions. There can never be a victory, for no person may conquer the sea. The emotions flow and color the mind's "reasonable" view of events. It is folly to think that the ocean will stop its roar, but the heart may hear the music within and rejoice in the splendor of the inevitable.

MARS: This is the planet of scientific action and insight. It is the force that tones the muscles and drives the sexual instincts to active expression. Mars is the most dynamic of all of the planets, and those heavily influenced by it will get things done, no matter what. If they cannot succeed they will destroy, for they can be ruthless. To a Mars native, everything presents a problem to be tackled and overcome. Mars can be a destructive, iconoclastic force, which when left to its own devices will attack and tear down old traditions and values. The sexual aspects of the planet are strikingly marked. For the Mars accented personality, sex is an almost overwhelming drive, not easily gratified. There is rarely any affection in their drive, as this is considered weakness. Badly aspected, its "macho" element becomes self-destructive. The ideas about behavior overwhelm any spontaneity in the personality and they become totally predictable.

MARS RULES: House of Aries.
DAY: Tuesday.
PLANTS: Biennials, basil, cactus, hops, mustards, nettle, onion, peppers, radish, thistle, tobacco, witch hazel. All plants with thorns, prickles or spines.
METAL: Iron.
FLOWER: Hollyhock.

 # The Star

INTERPRETATION: Only in silence can the voice of truth be heard. There is insight into the significance of events and things. Love abounds in the fullness of giving. This is the card of the good things of the earth.

SIGNIFICANCE: The star is the most massive of all physical forms, a sun in the making, a whole planetary system in the becoming, yet it appears as a tiny diamond in the sky. This is the level of solid illusion, where nothing is what it seems. Stars are diamonds. The Fool may touch, taste, smell, see, and hear, but will he ever know what it is that he experiences? The star represented on the card is Sirius, the dog star.

The woman pours the waters of the conscious and the unconscious upon the ground of dense matter. The contents of the mind are set free and consciousness is no longer shackled with concept and division, there is no longer that which is acceptable and that which is not acceptable.

INVERTED: There is loss brought about by stubbornness. Inability to release rigid belief structures can end in sickness of a systemic origin.

SEXUAL EXPRESSION: This is the card of those who have seen and done everything sexually, the sort of lover who accepts the hidden desires of the partner and allows them expression in a way that is not harmful. Great love will be given and the partner is open to receive it.

VALUE: Meditation.
COLOR: Violet.
TONE: A-Sharp. B-Flat.
DIRECTION: South above.

MEANING: The Fool's light, which illumines his darkness, is the result of disintegration, the steady crumbling of the fortress of the "I." As anything that burns, such as the sun, gives of light, so the disintegration of the Fool's point of view, the MY in myself, gives of a clarity that enables him to find his way in a spiritual light. The light of understanding, like

DESCRIPTION: The Star is the first card of the physical level, bright green in color with a bright geometrical border at the bottom. A woman is seated on a plynth. With her left hand she is pouring water for all to see. The right hand is pouring water secretly. Above her flies a macaw and to its left is the star. The star has eight points.

that of the star, probably takes a long time to reach other beings, and often reaches them only in a phantom state—as is the case with stars whose light we still see long after they themselves have burned out and are dark.

In meditation things become clear to the Fool. The sexual energy is used without exciting the sex centers themselves. The attention reaches out unquestioningly, and seeing and understanding are not actions separated by time. The oneness of existence is obvious to the Fool, simply because there is no separation. The Fool sees that all of his illusions have their root on this level, all of his thoughts are made of the stuff of this level, all of his perceptions are formed of responses to this, the material level. His senses did not deceive him; he deceived them. He ignored them, censured them, reevaluated them, all in the belief that he understood them better than did the body.

Fool, can you see how deceptive is the light of the star? Pour the waters of your consciousness upon the earth of your reasonable man. Empty the cups of the conscious and the unconscious and you will not lose a drop. From their waters will spring the tree of life. Its fruit is not knowledge, it is oneness. Turn the full light of consciousness (CIB) on your world, and the hidden shall be revealed. Secrets will be no more.

AQUARIUS: The Water Bearer. The key phrase for Aquarius is "to know," and it is this quest for awareness that often gives the natives of this sign their true humanity. Aquarius deals with friendships, group relationships, and original solutions to problems. Natives of this sign appear to be offhand and difficult to know, and their general attitude is one of independence. Rarely are they concerned with making an impression. Their attitude is generally cool, detached, even brusque. This is inevitably a protective device, mainly to prevent involvement. It is said that the Aquarian genius for invention springs from laziness. This same movement is what causes the native to surround himself with "labor-saving devices." The Aquarian fears criticism and is always underrating himself. They are in much demand; however, if any criticism is felt, real or imaginary, it awakens a stubborn streak that is almost suicidal in its intensity.

RULER: Uranus.
PLANTS: All plants having petals that are joined together or formed in one piece or having only one petal.
QUALITY: Masculine. Air.
BODY: Ankles and calves.
GEM: Blue Sapphire.

 # The Moon

CABAN ····· Shake off the ash ····················· 18

INTERPRETATION: This is the card of the psychic. It portends intuition that is unfailing, dreams that may fortell events, and the unfolding of latent powers. Unforseen problems can appear, the other side of a successful venture. Fame brings illusion. Body-knowing is the vibration of this card.

SIGNIFICANCE: They are wise who know themselves. The body has its own order, established over eons of interaction with the conditions that nature imposes. The mind that ignores the body will pay for it with atrification of its vehicle. The body is not just a car that must be kept running smoothly, oiled and supplied with the right fuel. It is the Fool's link with the REAL world, the source of all power (energy) within its closed system. It takes in what it needs, utilizes it, and rejects what it does not need. It is a holy (whole) piece of work, accomplishing such tasks, on a mundane basis, as would bring the mind into chaos. It is called an instrument of angels.

INVERTED: Deception will be recognized for what it is. Error will be uncovered and insta-

bility made stable. The practical will replace the ideal, but nothing risky will be undertaken. Reliable solutions are available for use.

SEXUAL EXPRESSION: This is the card of the "swinger," the person whose sexual life is on display for all to see. Only it is, of course, false, not real, an act. When the body is allowed to "feel," then order of a sexual nature comes about. Partners in the act are able to aid in the return of love, after lust and fear have almost destroyed it.

VALUE: Sleep.
COLOR: Red-violet.
TONE: B-Natural.
DIRECTION: South, below.

MEANING: The Fool's mental faculties have reached their limit. He must now discard all of the ideas and desires that have lead him this far. He must surrender completely to the totally non-rational influences of his inner light. If he does not he will be trapped here in sleep, the embrace of his ally, Death. He must give up entirely, regardless of the consequences, be

DESCRIPTION: A bright green card depicting the moon in its center. It has eight points in blue, surrounded by a white nimbus. Water, coming from the temperance card above, enters the card on the right side. Below are two volcanoes with flames coming from the tops. There are trees growing out of the brightly colored border at the bottom of the card.

they lunacy or madness. The Fool is in great danger. His journey is in peril. If he is caught in the glamor of the Moon, he will not be able to continue, for here he has to contend with fame. The world is beginning to heed him, for he has clarity of purpose that the world likes and will reward. His clarity must be overcome. He is caught in the body, knows how it works, and he is wise. His wisdom must be overcome. Wear and tear have made their mark on him and he is old. His old age must be overcome.

The Fool must burn the full light of consciousness totally to see his way, and when it is gone he must even shake off the ash (C'haban), for nothing may remain, nothing that the world may grasp and admire. He must be invisible, unable to be pressed into the service of fame or illusion.

The path is narrow, lit only by the volcanoes of renunciation and overcoming. He must not look back. At his side is his companion Death. It is too late for regrets and his endurance is taxed to the full. As in death, he can take nothing with him and must continue the journey alone. The prize is within his grasp . . . almost.

PISCES: The Fishes. The fishes that swim in opposite directions. This sign represents the attainment of universal consciousness at the end of the cycle, or complete degeneration and dissolution of all values into decay and death. In the sign of Pisces the fishes are tied together, indicating the difficulty of movement experienced by the natives of this sign. Generally, they are fearful of loss and want to hold on to their possessions and never let them out of their sight. They want to tie all their friends and acquaintences to them so that they may never escape. Pisces are easy going and resiliant, love entertaining, and welcome strangers with open arms. Natives of Pisces are the pursuers of dreams, often expressing a real difficulty in distinguishing between fantasy and reality. This often makes them self-indulgent and passive by nature. They are tenacious but not forceful. They affect little pride and can be slavish lovers.

RULER: Neptune.
PLANTS: Algae, pond scums and sea weeds, swamp plants such as mangrove and cattails.
QUALITY: Feminine. Water.
BODY: Feet.
GEM: Peridot.

The Sun

EZNAB ······ Perfection attained ····················· 19

DESCRIPTION: A large and elaborate yellow disk is in the center of the card. It is decorated with four points and four eggs. The four directions of north, south, east, and west are decorated with plumes. Above the sun on the left is the water from the temperance card and on the right the roots of the plant in the same card. At the bottom is the same geometric pattern as in all of the previous earth cards. There are trees growing from the design.

INTERPRETATION: Success and fruitfulness is the message of this card, contentment in the simple things of nature, triumph over the sterilizing effects of the sun. But be on guard; do not tarry too long in the sun.

SIGNIFICANCE: The sun is the symbol of psychic wholeness. It is the undivided union of the conscious and the unconscious that was poured upon the ground in the Star card, and which the sun now draws up and generously dispenses. The spark of life within each one of us first came from the sun, which sustains and nourishes us. The sun dispells all illusion. It burns openly for all to see and is the source of all we enjoy, yet we live in an age that finds fascination in its own doings and ignores the miracles around it.

INVERTED: This card is so strong that it loses nothing by being inverted.

SEXUAL EXPRESSION: Those who share the nature of this card enter into wholesome and vitalizing sexual relations with their partner. Love not lust excites the sun nature, and joy is taken in simple and loving behavior. This is the card of the innocent lover. It is the card of "the first time."

VALUE: Energy.
COLOR: Metallic gold.
TONE: D-Natural.
DIRECTION: South.

MEANING: Fruitfulness and sterility, the manifestations of the Sun, are but the two poles of a single effect. In moderation the sun fructifies the seed; in excess it sterilizes it. Two opposing effects from but a single force. The world of form and illusion no longer holds the Fool, for he has succeeded in stopping the synthesizing, illusory images that the mind uses to convey continuance in its world. Now he must use his own knowing, must take that which he needs and move on. The temptation is great to stay, playing in the sun. There is such delight in the warmth of the sun, the mind overloads with sensation. It wallows in mirage and eventually is lost to all recognition, gone forever to its own kingdom. The sun's energy fructifies and sterilizes.

The Fool has come safely through the land of the dead. Death is now his friend and companion, his advisor who warns him of danger. The Fool has emerged into new life and is reborn. His old self is dead, never to be again.

The energy used by the Fool up to this point was obtained from the excitation of the opposites. Now it is direct. Since there is no separation of the opposites, the energy is derived from the opposite functioning, when it is functioning, not from the movement between the opposites as they function. There is no division within the Fool because seeing is taking place and no opinion (idea) about that seeing is formed. The real world is real.

 **SUN**: The principal star of the solar system around which its planets revolve. The prime energy source for this galaxy. The Sun in a chart represents the strength of the ego, the vision the person holds of their own personality. It is "I AM." Sun people can be extremely vain, loving to dress up, always being found at center stage—not out of vanity but because they are genuinely interesting and deserving of the position. Susceptible to flattery, they are genuinely proud of their accomplishments and desire that they be appreciated.

SUN RULES: House of Leo.
DAY: Sunday.
PLANTS: Large, golden, round flowers with radiating petals, such as the sunflower. Fruit like oranges and saffron.
METAL: Gold.
FLOWER: Heliotrope. Helianthus. Gallardia.

Planet Venus

CAUAC ···· Divine nature is manifest ··········· 20

INTERPRETATION: There is renewed energy that signals a change in the way the world is viewed. Health improves and the mind brightens. There is a blossoming of confidence that enables a difficult work to reach completion. A peace is achieved and a timelessness perceived, so that the flow of things is seen and recognized. Success is achieved through a mixture of chance and care.

SIGNIFICANCE: This card bears the transcendent symbol for Feathered Serpent (Quetzalcoatl), the redeemer, the penitent who sacrificed himself in flame, journeyed eight days in the underworld, and arose transfigured as Venus, the love planet. Realization is achieved. Thought, with its fragmentation, has stopped. Love is, beauty is.

INVERTED: The opportunity is missed, the possibility for realization was not grasped, and thought has once more shattered the mirror of perception. Fragmentation is the movement of the mind.

SEXUAL EXPRESSION: A new perspective concening the whole of one's sexual activity

has opened up. There is a regeneration of energy and a freedom from the "animal" needs of the personality. Love has made its mark in this life. Everything is possible.

VALUE: Awareness.
COLOR: Blood red.
TONE: C-Natural.
DIRECTION: Center. North to South.

MEANING: Here the Fool achieves realization and his divine nature has become manifest. The twin aspects of the Serpent have joined in one body. The Fool has shaken off his old ways, his past is dead, and the period of growth, symbolized by the Sun, is at an end. The individual elements of the psyche have achieved full integration. The Serpent has learned to fly, for now the Fool travels his own path and leaves no trail. None may follow, there are no footprints to act as a guide, nothing is disturbed. All of the Fool's actions are complete and there is no drag from the past, no push into the future. THE FOOL IS FREE AT LAST. His work has just begun.

The Fool has become Feathered Serpent (Quet-

DESCRIPTION: A brilliantly colored blue and crimson Feathered Serpent fills the top half of the card. Behind the head is a white nimbus. To the left of the Serpent are the roots of the temperance plant. The forked tongue of the Serpent points downward between the same two volcanoes that appeared in the Moon card, and do not look so sinister now. At the bottom of the card is the same geometrical border seen in all of the earth cards.

zalcoatl). The myth has achieved reality. Feathered Serpent has returned to claim his kingdom, as he promised, and the great secret is revealed. Life exists in order that one may live and there is no meaning beyond living. When the Fool searched for meaning in life, he had expectations and reaped the reward of disappointment.

Life is not meaningless. It can never be meaningless, for it has never had a meaning. Since life has no meaning it is destructive for the Fool to search for meaning. Life simply is and has no purpose at all. There is no significance to life apart from living. From this all else follows.

PLUTO: Being the furthest planet, the Pluto influenced personality is a loner, an individual in the full meaning of the word (one, whole, cannot be separated). They tend to be shy and self-contained, so often apppear as strange and odd to their fellow humans. They can be cool, aloof, and distant, though always polite and of even temper. When Pluto is badly aspected in a chart, the isolation can be forced. There can be exile from loved ones, emmigration to distant and foreign lands. Pluto has a lot to do with criminal behavior and anti-social acts.

<u>PLUTO RULES</u>: House of Scorpio.
<u>DAY</u>: Night.
<u>PLANTS</u>: Almonds, blackwood, cress, blackberry, boxwood, garlic, geranium, horehound, horseradish, sasparilla, wormwood.
<u>METAL</u>: Plutonium.
<u>FLOWER</u>: Pitcher Plant.

 # Planet Earth

AHAU ·····One with divinity ························· 21

INTERPRETATION: Attainment and fulfillment. All things are possible. There is guaranteed success in whatever undertaking is embarked upon. There is a change in home or work, for the better.

SIGNIFICANCE: The journey is over and success has been achieved. The mind is no longer the tyrant of the Fool. He is integrated with all creation and there are no divisions between him and the world. The goal has been surpassed. There is oneness with divinity.

INVERTED: There has been no victory yet. The seeker loses his way. Fear has not been overcome.

SEXUAL EXPRESSION: This card tells how a man thinks of a woman sexually and how a woman thinks of a man sexually. It has meaning in the cards around it.

VALUE: Integrity.
COLOR: Blue-violet.
TONE: A-Natural.
DIRECTION: Center.

MEANING: The earth is a mystery. What the Fool sees is not all there is to the Earth, for it has bonds that tie it to all other planets and bonds that tie it to the sun. There is much more to the Earth, so much more in its vastness that it is endless. It is not separated from its kin, and neither is the Fool. The Earth is his mother. She nourishes and supports him. The journey is ended and just begun. The Tonal has been traversed, the Nagual entered into. There is oneness with divinity (AHAU) and separation is no longer possible, for it is not conceivable in the new cosmos of the Fool.

DESCRIPTION: The last card of the Higher Arcana and the five Earth cards. Primarily green in color, its center holds the symbol for the earth, a brown circle with eight trees growing on it. Lightning strikes and is grounded on the altar. On the altar is the cup that was in the hand of the temperance figure, but now there is incense pouring upwards out of it. On the right of the altar is the white flower of the Fool. The same geometrical border is at the bottom of the card, as in all of the earth cards.

Where there was neither heaven, nor earth,
Sounded the first word of the One.
It unloosed god-self from stone like silence
And it declared its divinity.

And all the vastness of eternity shuddered.
The God-word was a measure of grace and
God pierced and broke the backbone of the
   mountain.

Who was born then, who?
You know! for it is part of you to know.

It is the One. That which is lithe and subtle
In heaven, that One came into being.

              The Book of
              CHILAM BALAM.

SATURN: The Greek name for this planet was Chronos, and it means TIME. This is the planet of that which endures. Saturn stands for age, habit, custom, tradition, history, and ancient things preserved. There is little desire for innovation and change. This is *the* conservator. Personalities with Saturn well placed in their charts make excellent ecologists, museum curators, archeologists, researchers. Saturn usually is not prompt in its rewards. It tends to tear down, hinder, and destroy. The benefits of Saturn come late in life, for the destruction has built a fine foundation upon which an enduring success may be built.

SATURN RULES: House of Capricorn.
DAY: Saturday.
PLANTS: Woody perennials and plants that show annual rings and often have grey foliage or bark and insignificant flowers.
METAL: Lead.
FLOWER: Statice.

The Lower Arcana

All of the four suits of the Lower Arcana have cards numbered ten through one, and as well four Court Cards: Lord, Lady, Servant, and Warrior. The cards from ten to one indicate events that are concerned with the principal mode within which the particular suit functions. The Court cards, on the other hand, represent the people through whom this mode functions.

LORDS represent men, masculine functions, male powers and processes.

LADIES represent women, female functions, female powers and processes.

SERVANTS represent young persons of either sex, or the channel through which the aspect of the suit functions.

WARRIORS represent unmarried (available) persons of either sex, or the impetus, force, or thought behind the aspect of the particular suit. The warrior is dressed as the animal that represents the suit.

It is generally advised that when one selects a key card to represent a questioner, one should select a court card. For a married man or woman, select the Lord or Lady card; for an unmarried person of either sex, the Warrior card; for a boy or a girl, the Servant card. Conversely, when any of the court cards "turn up" in a spread and the situation indicates it, it can represent a person who has or will have a relationship to the enquirer, in whatever manner indicated by the rest of the spread.

If the last card of a spread inquiring about a legal matter turned up the Lord card, I would say that it represented the judge in the case and would advise a reading to find out his attitude towards the enquiry. Questions regarding the sex of Warrior and Servant cards that turn up in a spread must be decided either by the other cards or the nature of the question asked. Intuition may be of assistance.

A HANDY LIST FROM WHICH TIME, DIRECTION AND OTHER RELATIONSHIPS MAY BE DRAWN.

	STAFFS	SWORDS
Playing cards	CLUBS	SPADES
Court cards	LORD	WARRIOR
Realm	SPIRITUAL	MENTAL
Element	FIRE	AIR
Season	SUMMER	SPRING
Direction	EAST	NORTH
Color	ORANGE	YELLOW
Animal	JAGUAR	STAG
Place	MOUNTAIN	DESERT
Time	AFTERNOON	MORNING
Age	CHILD	YOUTH
Ally	PERSON	ANIMAL
State	LIGHT	GAS
Virtue	TRUTH	KNOWLEDGE
Psyche	INTUITION	INTELLECT
Sexuality	ACTIVE	CONSTANT
Art	CONCEPTION	DELINIATE
Painting	FORM	LINE
Music	TONE	MELODY
Orchestra	BRASS	WINDS
Humours	HOT	DRY
Psychology	EXTROVERTED	EXPANSIVE

CUPS	JADES
HEARTS	DIAMONDS
LADY	SERVANT
EMOTIONAL	PHYSICAL
WATER	EARTH
AUTUMN	WINTER
WEST	SOUTH
BLUE	GREEN
BIRD	MAN
COAST	FOREST
EVENING	NIGHT
MATURE	AGED
PLANT	MINERAL
LIQUID	SOLID
LOVE	WISDOM
FEELING	SENSES
VARIABLE	SENSUOUS
ABILITY	RESOURCES
COLOR	VOLUME
HARMONY	RHYTHM
STRINGS	PERCUSSION
WET	COLD
INTROVERTED	CONSERVATIVE

It can readily be seen from the chart that a great many relationships can be established and applied to the cross of the spread, on the appropriate directions.

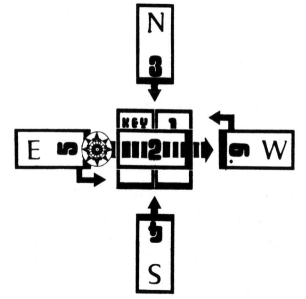

These related conditions are most useful and with practice an entire reading is possible from them alone. However it cannot be emphasized enough that none of the characteristics listed are better, superior, or more desirable than another; they simply represent the inclination, ability, or aspect best suited to that particular position on the spread.

If a Fire card turns up in the West, the place of water, obviously its energy is much more volatile. Fire and water produce steam and very quickly diminish each other's energy. On the other hand, a Fire card in the East is at home, and may be too strong unless it is controlled by a water card at home in the West.

When an Earth card turns up in the South and an Air card turns up in the North, it can be seen that mind and physical relationships are nicely balanced. With a Fire card in the West and a Water card in the East, it is more than likely that the Spiritual and Emotional aspects of a personality need to be brought into a harmonious relationship. If the same set of cards concerned a relationship with time, it could be said that Spring and Winter were favorable times for the endeavor, and that the Summer and Autumn ought to be avoided.

Again, practice will broaden your knowledge and supply you with a nearly endless set of circumstances through which your readings will gain depth and integrity.

There is a tradition in the tarot that relates back to numerology in which all the Lower Arcana cards are personified and given titles. This is a useful device that enables one to sum up each card in one word.

THE FOUR ONES:

Since these cards represent the spirit or essence of each suit, they are not listed as having separate values, for spirit is indivisible. They are said, however, to represent the four principal guardians of the earth, and they cover the dominions of these guardian angels (Devas).

STAFFS: The Lord of Asia (Japan, China, Tibet, india).

SWORDS: The Warrior of the Americas.

CUPS: The Lady of the Pacific (Oceania, Australia, New Zealand).

JADES: ·   The Servant of Africa, Europe, the Middle East and Russia.

THE FOUR TWOS:
STAFFS: Lord of Dominion.
SWORDS: Warrior of Peace.
CUPS: Lady of Love.
JADES: Servant of Change.

THE FOUR THREES:
STAFFS: Lord of Virtue.
SWORDS: Warrior of Sorrow.
CUPS: Lady of Abundance.
JADES: Servant of Work.

THE FOUR FOURS:
STAFFS: Lord of Completion.
SWORDS: Warrior of Truce.
CUPS: Lady of Luxury.
JADES: Servant of Power.

THE FOUR FIVES:
STAFFS: Lord of Strife.
SWORDS: Warrior of Defeat.
CUPS: Lady of Disappointment.
JADES: Servant of Worry.

THE FOUR SIXES:
STAFFS: Lord of Victory.
SWORDS: Warrior of Science.
CUPS: Lady of Pleasure.
JADES: Servant of Success.

THE FOUR SEVENS:
STAFFS: Lord of Valor.
SWORDS: Warrior of Futility.
CUPS: Lady of Debauch.
JADES: Servant of Failure.

THE FOUR EIGHTS:
STAFFS: Lord of Swiftness.
SWORDS: Warrior of Interference.
CUPS: Lady of Indolence.
JADES: Servant of Prudence.

THE FOUR NINES:
STAFFS: Lord of Strength.
SWORDS: Warrior of Cruelty.
CUPS: Lady of Happiness.
JADES: Servant of Gain.

THE FOUR TENS:

STAFFS: Lord of Oppression.

SWORDS: Warrior of Ruin.

CUPS: Lady of Satiety.

JADES: Servant of Wealth.

OUSPENSKY'S EXAMINATION OF THE METAPHYSICAL LINKS OF THE TAROT.

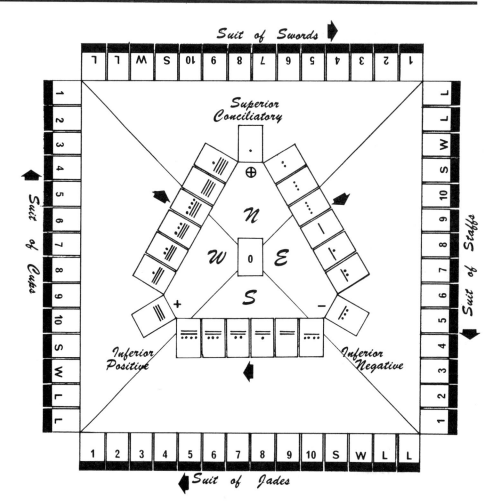

THE SPREAD RECOMMENDED BY P.D. OUSPENSKY for a meditation on the tarot is shown on the right. The entire deck is used to give an excellent picture of the relationship of the cards to each other and the relationship of the parts to the whole. Mr. Ouspensky gives this explanation of the spread:

... we have a representation of the relation between God, Man, and the Universe, or the relation between the world of ideas, the consciousness of man and the physical world.

The triangle is God (the Trinity) or the world of ideas, or the noumenal world. The point is the soul of man. The square is the visible, physical or phenomenal world.

*In essence Mr. Ouspensky is describing the **Tonal**, the world of form as represented by the square of the lower arcana, the **Nagual** is the triangle made of the higher arcana. The point in the center or the Fool card (0) is a person's consciousness at the center of **their** world of perception. The higher point of the triangle is the Sorcerer (1). At the East bottom is the negative pole (-) the cactus (8) the card of endurance the prime negative virtue, and the western pole (+) the prime positive virtue laughter, the Devil card. It is not difficult to see that endurance and laughter make the world of the Sorcerer a conciliation between all of the other positions represetned in the cards.*

The Path of Fire

DELINEATION OF THE SUIT OF STAFFS

All of the cards of the suit of Staffs deal with energy in its various manifestations. The Court cards stand for people and the way they use the energy available to them.

These are the cards of passion—not necessarily sexual, but the firy energy that sustains one in an enterprise that holds one caught within its bonds. Staffs indicate enthusiasm, ambition, and enterprise, not just in a worldly sense but throughout all of the levels of an inquiry. In occupation they deal wth the professionals—doctors, lawyers, teachers, and business people—and with the inquirer's station in life, particularly in regard to work involvement.

Staffs relate to the mystery of life and so are always depicted with a living leaf upon them. The mystery is the source of that life, and because they deal with life and energy they are also the cards that best indicate the state of the inquirer's nervous system. These are the cards of summer, the time of the year when the sun's energy is at its height, so they would also be used to indicate the zenith of a situation, the highest point to which an individual or situation, or the energy within both—may rise.

To recapitulate: the cards of the suit of Staffs deal with ENERGY, their time cycle is SUMMER, and they concern the occupation of the PROFESSIONAL. They deal with the nerves in sickness and health, and express the profundity of a person's spiritual understanding. Staffs are extroverted cards.

A man of an Aries temperament. This is the Lord of Fire and the spirit of persons and things, the highest manifestation of all things of the spirit when they are separated and examined apart from the whole. This is the card of the mediator, representing a man who is noble and courageous. He exhibits a virile and passionate nature and tends to be just in an enquiry. He is, however, slow to achieve a judgment. In a health inquiry this Lord represents healing through active examination and the laying on of hands.

SEXUAL ASPECTS: A dark and attractive man, well-built, tending to be tall. He could be an unexpected sexual relationship that blossoms into an enduring one.

REVERSED: A person who tends to need violence attached to their sex. A cold calculating person who can make a satisfactory partner in the act, but does not supply any of the warmth and affection that the partner desires.

A woman of a Leo temperament. This is the Lady of Fire, the feminine aspect of the spirit as it manifests itself in separation from the whole. She represents the passive energy qualities such as endurance and peace, energy that manifests through the lady of the earth, energy stored in oil, coal and plants. She represents the sustenance in food, and when there is a health problem she represents the energy of healing itself.

SEXUAL ASPECTS: A woman of great charm, loving and friendly. She is the dark, exotic beauty of Song and legend. She is sexually magnetic and tends to be impassioned by her man. She is generally faithful, having little need to be promiscuous for she tends to generate within her partner the type of response that satisfies her.

REVERSED: A jealous woman of insecure and unstable passions. If the partner's response is not to her satisfaction, she will unhesitatingly take a lover, usually keeping such action a secret.

A young person of a Sagittarian temperament. The Servant represents the manner in which or channel through which the energy manifests itself. He principally is a message (by telephone, telegraph or post) that propels the inquirer into energy-charged situations. He represents a person who is dynamic and enthusiastic. In a situation concerning health, this card denotes a drug or medicine; it is the stimulating that speeds up the metabolism, blood flow or heart beat.

SEXUAL ASPECTS: A person of slight but vigorous build, a messenger, postman, telephone repair person, someone who is in service and in a position to bring news of a lover, or perhaps to be that lover. A young gigolo or hustler.

REVERSED: A breaker of hearts; an indecisive or reluctant lover. A young lover who is a sexual gossip, unable to still a boasting tongue about matters best kept secret. Untrustworthy and unstable.

The impetus behind the fire of the spirit, energy, the Warrior card is the movement of the energy involved in any situation. It has a sudden impetuous nature and is subject to disturbing influences. The Warrior brings unrest; and in matters of psychological health, he is the "stirring of the bottom of the pot", the probing into the latent energy of a situation that brings distress but in retrospect was worth it.

SEXUAL ASPECTS: A dark Latin type, very attractive to women, but somewhat unstable in his affections. Always searching for sexual companions, the nature tends to be promiscuous but generous.

REVERSED: Has the capacity to create conflict and rivalry. Quarreling over sexual matters. The type of friend or lover who can become brutal and jealous over trivial matters.

THE 10 OF STAFFS:

DESCRIPTION: A man sitting in a sheltering circle of staffs. He has his eyes shut and his arms folded across his chest in a protective way. Brightly colored birds flit about in the air.

INTERPRETATION: The wonders and mysteries of life surround one. There are messengers all around, but one has eyes that are closed to all of the possibilities. There are benefits everywhere; all one has to do is open up.

REVERSED: A glut of possibilities, making it impossible to see a path through the world. Involvement in contradiction and intrigue.

SEXUAL EXPRESSION: Experiencing difficulty in satisfying many sexual partners. Women have worries over possible unwanted pregnancies. Excessive sex leading to veneral disease.

THE 9 OF STAFFS:

DESCRIPTION: A warrior is returning after a fight, wounded but content with the victory. The warrior has lost one of the staffs, but he isn't worried. He has others.

INTERPRETATION: The person has fought before and there is more to come. He has strength when opposed, and is able to defend adequately against whatever adversity there may be. There can be delays and obstinacy, obstacles and adversity to overcome.

REVERSED: Showing a weakness of character that manifests as unpreparedness and unwillingness to fight until it is too late.

SEXUAL EXPRESSION: Relief at being able to satisfy the partner in a clandestine affair. Competence with a person very beautiful and intimadating. Feeling one proved oneself, but never again.

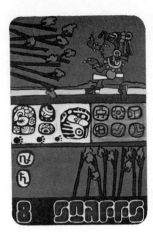

THE 8 OF STAFFS:

DESCRIPTION: A man is shown pointing at a group of staffs, as if telling them what to do. He points upward, indicating a higher authority.

INTERPRETATION: The path of activity in an undertaking. Action and swiftness in approaching a goal. Speed towards an end that promises happiness.

REVERSED: Internal quarrels and disputes. Difficulties with authorities. Qualms of conscience over methods used to achieve goals.

SEXUAL EXPRESSION: A love affair is a strong possibility. There could also be a change of sexual tastes, a change in sexual partners, or sexual decisions hurriedly made. Badly aspected, it indicates jealousy, quarrels over roles played in the affair.

THE 7 OF STAFFS:

DESCRIPTION: A warrior is dressed for battle, and with one staff he opposes six others. He has a shield and is dressed as a jaguar.

INTERPRETATION: Holding one's own against adversity. Strong competition in business. In the past it is a battle already won. In the future it is a battle shaping up. Negotiations are difficult but successful.

REVERSED: Caution against indecision. Difficulties will pass you by but beware of others attempting to take advantage.

SEXUAL EXPRESSION: Competition for the desired partner is overcome by sexual aggressiveness. Fights for sexual mastery. Impotence or distress caused by the sexual demands made upon one.

THE 6 OF STAFFS:

DESCRIPTION: A man dressed as a victor points to a staff decorated with a wreath of victory.

INTERPRETATION: This is the card of good news and victory over a difficult situation. There will be increased harmony in relationships. Advances will be made in a chosen profession.

REVERSED: A delay in just rewards. News of the victory of another. There is apprehension over insolence from the winner. Disloyalty.

SEXUAL EXPRESSION: Waiting is over; the desired partner seeks gratification. There is sexual mastery and fulfillment. Reversed, there is more waiting and even greater insecurity. A treacherous lover takes another partner.

THE 5 OF STAFFS:

DESCRIPTION: A person seems to be the center of an attack by at least two others. The combat is vigorous but may only be a game.

INTERPRETATION: Strenuous competition in one's chosen field of endeavor. Courage in the fight can bring gain and reward. The possibility of a lawsuit or problems with neighbors.

REVERSED: New opportunities are available and manifest as harmony in one's affairs. A desire to help others with practical aid. Watch out for trickery, disputes with attorneys, etc.

SEXUAL EXPRESSION: Foreplay in sex assumes more importance than the act itself. The excessive involvement with fantasy leads to an inability to perform the act. A loss of virility caused by quarreling. Reversed, a partner's excessive demands can be fulfilled.

THE 4 OF STAFFS:

DESCRIPTION: The seed of the maize (corn), if fertile, springs to life, protected by a canopy bearing an image of the sun and supported by four staffs.

INTERPRETATION: This is the card of beauty and harmony in one's private life. It can mean a patron or a person who helps one grow and achieve success, refuge, and peace.

REVERSED: There is no change in its meaning. Taking pleasure in the beauties of the natural world.

SEXUAL EXPRESSION: A sense of security with one's chosen partner. In marriage it can mean conception of a child long desired. Satisfaction with one's self and the partner's response.

THE 3 OF STAFFS:

DESCRIPTION: A prosperous person, standing on land surrounded by water. He grasps two staffs firmly, and the third, although in the water, is within easy reach.

INTERPRETATION: Practical people can help one and may even form a partnership. There is enterprise, and business affairs flourish. There is strength and cooperation in commerce and profession.

REVERSED: The business venture is a success but the profit realized is a disappointment. There is an end to adversity, but it does not bring a reward with it.

SEXUAL EXPRESSION: Probblems of passivity and frigidity are overcome. The fires of passion are lit and a new freedom is experienced during the sex act. Inverted there is masturbation instead of union, satisfaction but no reward.

THE 2 OF STAFFS:

DESCRIPTION: A person who is in the professions stands on a promontory looking outward. He holds in one hand a globe, and in the other he holds a staff. On either side of him is a snow-covered mountain.

INTERPRETATION: On one hand are riches and fortune, on the other suffering and disease. There is sadness amid plenty. An endeavor may bear fruit too early. It eventually withers on the vine.

REVERSED: A good beginning can end in domination by another. There can be an awakening of surprise and wonder at the turn of events.

SEXUAL EXPRESSION: One's wildest fantasies are realized but have a hollow and empty feel to them. The sex act can be devoid of excitement. Passions are cooled and desires are thwarted.

THE 1 OF STAFFS:

DESCRIPTION: A bowl containing flame and fire overflows in its vigor. A staff is surrounded by flame but does not burn. A jaguar rests peacefully on its front paw.

INTERPRETATION: Creation, invention, enterprise, and all the powers that are the result of these. It can mean a birth in the family, or at one's work. Virility behind the creative act. Inheritance.

REVERSED: Clouded joy, in that a good idea is not appreciated or is simply ahead of its time. A lack of determination that causes disinterest in others and a setback for the project in mind.

SEXUAL EXPRESSION: Virility and fertility. Exciting sexual escapades, with childlike enjoyment. A mindless act of insensitivity. This is the card of castration and circumcision, impotency and frigidity.

The Path of Air
DELINEATION OF THE SUIT OF SWORDS

The cards of the suit of Swords deal with courage, ambition, force and aggression. They are the cards of competition and individuality. The court cards stand for people and individuals who have power and authority over us.

These are the cards of the mind and intellect, perpetually cutting down, dissecting and inquiring. Swords represent action in the world. They generally tend to be negative in their effect, for swords and knives are not the gentlest way of solving problems. Swords may be characterized as "Might is Right." There is an aspect of brotherhood about them, such as comrades in arms. Professionally these are the cards of bureaucrats, the military, surgeons (those who heal with the knife), critics, tax collectors, and the like.

Swords are the cards of masculine energy, that which pierces and separates. They are the cards of the left hemisphere of the brain, the examiner of minute detail. This energy is lineal in that it flows only in one direction, from the past to the future.

As a health indicator, they relate to the lungs and the throat, also the skin and the nose.

To recapitulate, the suit of Swords deals with the mind in all its aspects. The time cycle is Spring and the cards concern the occupations that exercise authority, military, critics and teachers. Air cards deal with the lungs, nose and throat, also the skin. The Swords are expansive cards.

A man of a Gemini temperament. This is the Lord of Air, and he is a judge, a decider, and an impartial reviewer of evidence. He is the highest manifestation of the things of the mind, with the power to command life or death in a situation. A man of black and white, there are very few shades of grey within his view of the world. He is a firm decision maker, whether with friends or enemies, but his failings are overcautiousness and a rather suspicious nature. When he is clear and certain, his advice can be most helpful and full of good ideas. He represents healing through the knife.

SEXUAL ASPECTS: A mature man with dark hair and eyes. He manifests great sexual potency, passion, and erotic arousal. He represents the homosexual in military power. Sexual authority is his command.

REVERSED: He represents sexual aberrations such as flagellation and humiliation, bondage and pederasty.

A woman of Libra temperament. This is the Lady of Air, the feminine aspect of the mental processes, representing the balancing and coordinating abilities. She is confident and perceptive in her dealings with others. She represents widows or women who are alone in the world, those who have children and no husband. The Lady is a keen observer, and this can manifest as cruelty to others. She can be sly and deceitful, can manifest malice and bigotry, and can be a terrible gossip.

SEXUAL ASPECTS: A woman who separates lovers, who enjoys breaking up affairs. She often exhibits tendencies towards lesbian behavior and action. She can be frigid and use sex as a weapon to injure others.

REVERSED: A deceitful woman who presents herself as a virgin. All of the virtues she manifests are false: chastity, sensuality and love. She suppresses her desires to gain power over others.

A young person of an Aquarian temperament. This card is called the Servant of the Rushing Winds, and it manifests the qualities of things that do not manifest themselves in the open and are underhanded, though not necessarily evil (such as spying). The servant is graceful and dexterous, shows understanding and diplomacy in situations requiring a sensitive hand.

SEXUAL ASPECT: A young person with brown hair and eyes, manifesting a strong curiosity in the sex lives of others. This is the card of a voyeur and one who secretly indulges in perusing erotic literature.

REVERSED: A person who becomes depressed about sexual matters, who suffers from premature ejaculation. Those who practice evil sexual behavior.

An unmarried person with brown hair and eyes. He shows skill, bravery, and a decided penchant for rushing headlong into situations that could do with a bit more consideration. This is the card of resistance and opposition. It is the destruction caused by war. This card can signify the death of a situation or person when combined with other cards. It is the card of fatality.

SEXUAL ASPECT: A person who is cold, efficient and forceful in carrying out sexual escapades. A person who conquers their sexual foe.

REVERSED: Imprudent, impulsive sexual behavior that leads to complications and trouble. Extravagance in wooing the partner.

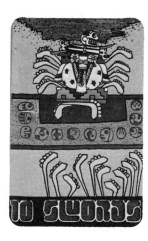

THE 10 OF SWORDS:

DESCRIPTION: A mortuary bundle prepared for burial, with the shin bones and the skull on top of it. The bundle is surrounded by ten swords.

INTERPRETATION: There can be sudden misfortune, sadness and tears. There can be defeat in a legal battle or war. This is not a card of violent death but more of pain and loss.

REVERSED: The overthrow of negative forces and the strength to succeed once more. There can be profit and better health, but it won't last.

SEXUAL EXPRESSION: Trouble in the genitals, sickness and cutting. A hypersensitivity to role playing that leads to impotence. Reversed, there is sexual success of a temporary nature only.

THE 9 OF SWORDS:

DESCRIPTION: A person deathly white in color sits before an altar on which are resting six swords. On the ground are another three. They all point towards the supplicant.

INTERPRETATION: When combined with other cards, this is the card of death. It also is the card of miscarriage. All the miseries are manifest in this card: deception, failure, disappointment, and despair.

REVERSED: With patience and forbearance there is healing, though suspicion and doubt still cloud the air. Imprisonment is possible.

SEXUAL EXPRESSION: This is the card of enforced celibacy, undesired pregnancy, and sexual shame. It is also the card of the loss of virginity. There is a conflict of morals and desires that may put an end to the sexual life of the inquirer.

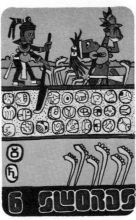

THE 8 OF SWORDS:

DESCRIPTION: A woman, arms bound and eyes blindfolded, walks away from a temple with a mortuary bundle under its roof. She is surrounded by four swords. The other four swords surround the bundle.

INTERPRETATION: The person on the card is slowly but surely making her way out of diversity. There is sickness, crisis, and conflict, still present but on the decline.

REVERSED: There is a freedom from restrictions beginning to be felt, but one is still too weak to avail oneself of it wholly. A person in prison will be released.

SEXUAL EXPRESSION: This is the card of domination by someone who is sexually perverted. There can be abuse, even slavery ending in confinement. Reversed, there appears a way out of trouble.

THE 7 OF SWORDS:

DESCRIPTION: A warrior dressed ceremonially carries a shield with an eye in the center and four swords he has stolen.

INTERPRETATION: There has been the failure of a plan and it causes annoyance. There is unreliability, and a betrayal of confidence that leads to quarreling and vexation. There is wishing and hoping that things would be different.

REVERSED: Good advice and counsel are offered and should not be refused. Something that was stolen is returned secretly.

SEXUAL EXPRESSION: Confidence in one's sexual ability is weak. There is the feeling of betrayal by the partner, even suspicion of extramarital affairs. These suspicions are unreal yet very hard to deal with. A talk with trusted friends will settle matters.

THE 6 OF SWORDS:

DESCRIPTION: A man in a canoe holds a newborn infant on high. He is surrounded by swords but does not seem worried. The boat is guided by a young man. The water is a clear blue. The far bank is visible.

INTERPRETATION: This is the card of journeys, both by travel and away from adversity. New things are happening and clarity of mind is ahead.

REVERSED: The postponement of a journey. A public confession. There is no immediate way out of present difficulties. Undesired publicity over personal matters.

SEXUAL EXPRESSION: This is the card of casual intercourse, of strangers meeting in the night. Reversed, it is a declaration of love or even a proposal of marriage.

THE 5 OF SWORDS:

DESCRIPTION: A man dressed to celebrate victory clutches the swords of his adversary, who is kneeling and is in tears.

INTERPRETATION: Conquered by unfair means, a hollow victory. There is failure and defeat that is hard to take, a humiliating defeat by very questionable methods. Something could be stolen.

REVERSED: Very little change from the above. Maybe things won't be quite so rough, but there is no guarantee of that; in fact, things may become worse.

SEXUAL EXPRESSION: A loss of sexual partner, or a loss of potency. This is the card of rape, dishonor, or sexual deviation.

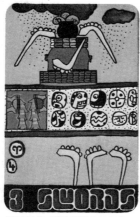

THE 4 OF SWORDS:

DESCRIPTION: A man quietly balances a sword, while three others hang in the air above him. He does not seem perturbed at all.

INTERPRETATION: This is a card of retreat and repose, of the thoughtfulness that brings balance to a situation. A convalescence after illness or unrelenting work. A warning of the need for caution and discretion in one's activities.

REVERSED: The circumspection in dealings that may appear as wise administration to some people, and as avarice and lack of caution to others. Reversed, this is the card of social unrest.

SEXUAL EXPRESSION: This is the card of the sexual bigot, the person who is hung-up about sex. It can mean retreat from sexual excess or simply a lack of interest in sexual matters.

THE 3 OF SWORDS:

DESCRIPTION: A heart is placed in the center of an altar, surrounded by three swords. There are dark clouds in the sky, and it is raining.

INTERPRETATION: Quarrels and separation are on the horizon. The eternal triangle leads inevitably to upheaval in one's personal life. This card also portends civil and political strife.

REVERSED: The general meaning is the same as above, but less extreme. There is less disorder, and less loss that follows.

SEXUAL EXPRESSION: Heartbreak and the end of sexual companionship. One's sexual life is in upheaval and disarray. There is sexual incompatibility and a confusion of sexual interests.

THE 2 OF SWORDS:

DESCRIPTION: A woman sits blindfolded in front of a rocky stream. She holds two swords. The Sword in her left hand points down and the one in the right hand points up.

INTERPRETATION: There is a balance in personal relationships which seems more like a stalemate. There is indecision and could even be trouble ahead if one does not attend to things directly.

REVERSED: There is release, but the direction seems to be wrong. Falsehood and duplicity can be ahead and caution should be counseled, for things will not be easy to overcome.

SEXUAL EXPRESSION: Compatibility in relationships brings its reward of warmth and affection. There is a tenderness and intimacy rarely experienced before. Reversed, all of the above is in ruin.

THE 1 OF SWORDS:

DESCRIPTION: Currents of air rush around a sword that seems to be growing out of the ground. There are clear white clouds in the sky, and the animal of the suit, the stag, is pictured, head only.

INTERPRETATION: Swords are hardly ever beneficent, but the ace card represents partition, the birth of a child. The surfacing of a leader, who will lead the people out of darkness. The clash of opposites. The force of Love and Hate, the double-edged sword.

REVERSED: The same as above, but exaggerated. Paths that lead to the light revert to darkness once more. The leader entrenches himself and holds to power. Overkill is the active force in this position.

SEXUAL EXPRESSION: Force used to gain sexual ends. The "casting couch" and the secretary who must "please" her boss are aspects of this card. The results are always disastrous, and often violent as well.

The Path of Water

DELINEATION OF THE SUIT OF CUPS

The cards of the suit of Cups deal with happiness, beauty, fertility, and equilibrium. These are the cards of partnerships and the merging of differences. The court cards stand for people and individuals whose power is in charm and charisma, who win us over to their way by example and love.

These are the cards of the emotions, always flowing, changeable and deep. Cups represent the feelings that we have about the world. They also represent the subconscious, that part of our perception that we have difficulty facing. Since they represent water, these cards are always involved in some movement, towards finding a balance. Water must always find its own level. The key to a contented life is to have the emotions in balance. Professionally these are the cards of the entertainer, the experimenter, and those who heal through potions (homeopaths) and involvement, such as therapists.

Cups are the cards of Feminine energy, that which combines and expands. They are the cards of the right hemisphere of the brain, the unifier of diverse perceptions. This energy is multi-directional, that is, flows equally in all directions, and is not concerned with the past or future except as part of now. As an indicator of health, it covers the psychological and psychosomatic aspects of one's life.

To recapitulate, the suit of Cups deals with the EMOTIONS and all of their complications. The time cycle of cups is AUTUMN. The occupations are ENTERTAINERS as authority figures (the passive dominant), advertising and artist types. Cups cover PSYCHOSOMATIC illnesses, love sickness and the like. The Cups are introverted cards.

A man of a Cancer temperament. This is the Lord of water. He rules in a kind and considerate way, and is not afraid of the responsibility he carries. He is the manifestation of the emotions, and his power is that of merging, compromise, and persuasion. This is the ruler or judge who is concerned with the well-being of his subjects; he has compassion and mercy towards those under his command. The weakness is indolence, self-indulgence, and decadence. When well-aspected, the Lord of Cups does not display his emotional side but exhibits a calm and endearing aspect and enjoys quiet, peaceful power.

SEXUAL ASPECTS: A man of fair complexion with hazel eyes. He feels a responsibility towards sexual partners, and does not shirk his duties as a provider. He is an obliging lover.

REVERSED: He can be selfish, inconsiderate as a partner, a liar and seducer who uses his power in a childish way to gain sex.

A woman of a Scorpio temperament. A beautiful woman with a fair complexion, she has passion and commitment, yet seems to lack common sense in her dealings with others. She tends to be poetic and artistic in an inward sense. She dresses with flair, tends to be talkative (but not objectionably so), and is more entertaining than anything else. She is gentle, good-natured and happy most of the time. Badly aspected, she can be perverse, unreliable, moody, and allow her imagination to get out of control. She can become bitter.

SEXUAL ASPECTS: A good wife and a loving mother. She is a romantic who serves her lover well. She makes a perfect mistress.

REVERSED: She can be a nag and a castrator, using duty as a weapon. Her love of luxury can bring her paramour to the brink of ruin.

SERVANT

A young person of a Pisces temperament. A good and helpful person who will aid the questioner. Though inclined to be dreamy, there is courage here when it is needed. A quiet and studious person, inclined to acting and occupations requiring an ability to imagine and make concrete that imagination. Reversed, this card is inclined towards a pedantic behavior, a demanding, childish temperament, and an inability to tell fantasy from reality, a person who thinks their taste is the only real standard by which things are to be judged.

SEXUAL ASPECTS: The card of effeminate young men, and young girls who are excessively feminine in their demeanor. It is also the card of those who do sexual service for money or entertainment.

REVERSED: Those who take sexual advantage of others by the use of drugs, marijuana, alcohol, etc. The gay seducer who takes advantage of the weakness of others.

WARRIOR

An unmarried person with fair hair and eyes, one who is intelligent and warm, a good dancer, and an excellent socializer who knows how to please others. He is a romantic with his feet on the ground, who knows how to praise another without going too far. This is the card of the musician. He is also the agent of emotional impacts in the life of the questioner. Reversed, he is the "con man," a tricky and deceitful person.

SEXUAL ASPECTS: The person who knows how to propose a sexual liaison and present it as exciting and passionate. An exciting and refreshing lover.

REVERSED: One who takes advantage. A wife seducer, a cunning person intent on rape and the seduction of virgins.

THE 10 OF CUPS:

DESCRIPTION: A happy family scene. A well-to-do family with food, clothing, shelter, and a child, all they need for a pleasant life. The sun is in the sky and everyone seems content.

INTERPRETATION: Peace and contentment, repose of the heart, love and friendship—all are in this card. A balanced, full life with needs supplied and continuance assured.

REVERSED: Children turn against the parents and reject the old values. Confusion and loss of old friendships. A family quarrel is possible. There may be damage to property or good name.

SEXUAL EXPRESSION: A sexual union that is gratifying and fulfilling. Sex that is invigorating and lots of fun, with no guilt felt. Reversed, there is sexual wantonness and debauchery. Hysteria becomes a way of achieving desires. The worship of genitals.

THE 9 OF CUPS:

DESCRIPTION: A well-dressed, obviously rich woman makes offerings in thanksgiving for blessings received; also to ask that things continue to be good, for she has lost one cup (no great loss, yet a loss no less).

INTERPRETATION: There is assured material success and advantage in social position that can be used. The future seems certain. A love of beautiful things and the ability to purchase them.

REVERSED: There are mistakes and imperfections induced by the isolation that money and lack of struggle can bring about. There can be an overindulgence in food and drink.

SEXUAL EXPRESSION: This card denotes a love of sensual pleasure and sexual stimulation. It can point to an overindulgence leading to sickness, and boredom over sexual practices. Unfulfillment.

THE 8 OF CUPS:

DESCRIPTION: A man wanders, as though looking for something. He holds a staff (the only one in the cups). It is night and the moon looks on. He has crossed many obstacles.

INTERPRETATION: There is disappointment with one's present lifestyle. Material success has become meaningless and there is searching for a deeper level of understanding.

REVERSED: A turning away from the spiritual approach. A reaction to unfulfillment on a less material level. Materialism is indicated.

SEXUAL EXPRESSION: This is the card of the masturbator and enjoyer of autoerotic practices. There is a shyness and timidity in approaching others that seems to shut the others out. Reversed, it is the card of bisexuality and group sex. Hedonism is indicated.

THE 7 OF CUPS:

DESCRIPTION: A man holds a flaming jewel on high, either placing it on the altar or taking it off the altar, which is crowded with all manner of exciting things.

INTERPRETATION: This is the card of attainment and wishes granted, though it gives no guarantee of permanence.

REVERSED: Shows a will to accomplish the desired goal. There is the selection of a particular path and a clear following up of whatever success becomes apparent.

SEXUAL EXPRESSION: Dreams of a sexual nature are indicated, in which the imagination is allowed to run riot. Sexual fantasy is allowed to hold sway, with themes of mastery over others and domination. Badly aspected, it can mean violent sexual practice or excessive fantasy, leading to a failure in sex with others.

THE 6 OF CUPS:

DESCRIPTION: A well-dressed older man is presenting a gift to a young girl, who seems pleased to receive it. Both seem content.

INTERPRETATION: Contentment and enjoyment that comes from the past. An enduring friendship will be established. There could be gifts from long time admirers, possibly an inheritance.

REVERSED: A reversal of the roles is indicated, and a gift will be, or should be, given to a younger person who is liked and admired by the questioner. An inheritance is not as large as one hoped for.

SEXUAL EXPRESSION: This is a card of sexual joy and contentment. There is sex with a "sweet young thing" who finds needs fulfilled in the questioner. Maybe love letters out of the past show up. Reversed, it indicates a desire for a change of partner, worries over aging,

THE 5 OF CUPS:

DESCRIPTION: A man clouded in depression walks along a path. His arms are folded in a self-protecting manner. In the background is a temple. A rich green field lies before him.

INTERPRETATION: Three cups are overturned, yet two remain. All is not lost. There can be disillusionment over the turn of events and regret at the way things were handled.

REVERSED: There is the courage to overcome the obstacles or loss. Hope is renewed and friends come to the rescue. One must beware of projects that may be doomed from the start.

SEXUAL EXPRESSION: A bitter marriage is indicated. There could also be the breaking up of a marriage, with struggles over custody and property. Temporary impotence and difficulties due to the emotional pressure of circumstances. Sexual frustration and teasing.

THE 4 OF CUPS:

DESCRIPTION: A god is in the air, dispensing favors. In one hand is lightning (energy) and the other pours water (sustenance), but the man is not open to it. Even his cup is turned down.

INTERPRETATION: There are blessings all around, but we are not open to receive them. There is a wariness about and aversion to becoming involved in things. Problems are of an imaginary nature.

REVERSED: A new source of energy has become available. New friends and novelties present themselves. New ambitions make new goals possible. A desire to achieve success is manifest.

SEXUAL EXPRESSION: Discontent and satiety with the sexual act. There is boredom with and a shutting out of a loving partner who is unable to help. Reversed, the partner can find a way through and once more joy enters the relationship.

THE 3 OF CUPS:

DESCRIPTION: Three young people are shown and all seem contented. One has a cup that is overflowing and is about to fill the cups of the others.

INTERPRETATION: Unsuspected talents are realized. There is an agreeable conclusion to things underway. There is solace and healing if unhappiness or sickness is present.

REVERSED: One must pay the price for past indulgences. Talent is not appreciated and abundance turns to waste. A cheerful payment of past debts will mitigate the circumstances now coming to pass.

SEXUAL EXPRESSION: One is in great demand sexually. The bull is in clover. Sexual talents are appreciated and life bestows its bounty. In a reversed card there are excesses and depravity, also a loss of virility. Things are not irretrievable.

THE 2 OF CUPS:

DESCRIPTION: Two lovers meet under a shelter and pledge their faithfulness to each other.

INTERPRETATION: This is the card of lovers. There is a balance of complimentary forces, a union of friends and lovers. Partners in business discover a harmony that is beneficial, both financially and personally.

REVERSED: This card loses none of its meaning by being reversed.

SEXUAL EXPRESSION: There are no demands made by either partner. They have discovered each other and find fulfillment in each other, both sexually and as friends. There is always pleasure in each other's company. No restrictions in sexual matters.

THE 1 OF CUPS:

DESCRIPTION: A pleasantly decorated cup, over which hovers a hummingbird, having drunk its fill. Bright, airy flowers decorate the card, and water is seen flowing freely.

INTERPRETATION: There is nourishment and abundance for all to share. Love, joy, and beauty abound. Life is full and bountiful. The good things of life.

REVERSED: A wall is built, through fear of not being worthy. There is a fear of whole-hearted commitment to life and too much remembrance of past difficulties. There is revolution.

SEXUAL EXPRESSION: Love is discovered hiding within oneself or one's partner. What had just been sex for the sake of sex now blossoms into a new appreciation of the worth of each other. Reversed, it indicates sterility and frigidity, a loss of desire for the partner, or a downright refusal.

The Path of Earth
DELINEATION OF THE SUIT OF JADES

The cards of the suit of Jades are perhaps the most mundane of all of the cards, since they deal with our work, personal resources and business matters. The court cards stand for people whose authority is undoubted, leaders swept to power by universal acclaim. Gurus, teachers, and dictators are also represented here.

Jades are the cards of physical existence, the solid, real world of nature. They are our actions in the real world and the effects that our actions have upon that world. They are the conscious world as well, the order that we accept as "normal." These cards are of the earth: giving, practical, conservative. Their virtues are patience and industry, for the earth is bountiful when husbanded with love and care. The earth is patient with mistakes and does not offer swift retribution, but allows time for healing to take place. The earth's healing is through the humours,

hot and cold, wet and dry, all in their proper balance. The cards also deal with the sex life of a person as it affects their outlook on life.

Jades are the cards of conservative energy, that is, they balance times of plenty with times of scarcity. It is a declining energy, so tends to hold itself back. It is retiring and conducive of sleep. It governs healing with herbs and plants and illnesses that are caused by an imbalance of natural resources, minerals and vitamins.

To recapitulate, the suit of Jades deals with MATERIAL existence, action in the world and the responses to those actions. Its time cycle is WINTER. The occupations are CRAFTSMEN, carpenters, potters, weavers, and the like. Jades deal with illnesses caused by imbalance or systemic illnesses. They are paternal and authoritarian. Jades are conservative.

A man of a Taurus temperament. This is the Lord of Earth, a conservative, authoritarian gentleman. A banker, or university professor, with great facility in mathematics and the abstract sciences. He could be a spiritual leader. He is a man who wears worldly success well, and his power comes from the knowledge of orderly progression. He sees things in steps and so brings them to fruition. Reversed, he is inclined towards corrupt practice and a crystalization of thought and reason. The book of rules guides him and he sees no reason to change. He can be rigid and unforgiving.

SEXUAL ASPECTS: A dark man with dark eyes. He is an affectionate companion and a good provider. He uses reason to persuade others to supply sexual favors.

REVERSED: A person who buys sex and demands his money's worth. A seducer of young people through bribes, a corruptor of their moral values.

A woman of a Virgo temperament. She is the Earth mother, the cornucopia of bountiful harvests. The Lady is thoughtful and highly intelligent. She has a profound sense of security about her, which enables her to indulge in opulence and luxury, and is wealthy with the earth's bounty. Reversed, she becomes dependent and develops a suspicious and mistrusting nature. Harrassed by a fear of failure, she is no longer creative or giving of nature. She hoards things, awaiting evil times.

SEXUAL ASPECTS: A beautiful woman, a good and guiding mother. The Lady has great freedom and expresses it sexually in generosity and largess. She is a lover of pleasure and titillation.

REVERSED: The Lady is licentious and vicious, unsatiated and always in a state of anxiety over sexual matters.

A young person of a Capricorn temperament. A person who wins laurels for study and loves learning for its own sake, who is open to new ideas and is good at getting them accepted by others, who has a thoughtful, open mind and listens to the opinions of others Reversed, this person can be wasteful and develop a taste for luxury. The card can bring unfavorable news.

SEXUAL ASPECTS: A pubescent boy or girl, caught in daydreams about sex. A person who finds a way through the maze of sexual information and misinformation to the sexual act.

REVERSED: A person of rebelious tendencies, whose sexual inclination is a protest against the established values. A gay person or bisexual person.

A black-haired dark-eyed person who is unmarried or available. A responsible and trustworthy person who can be of great service to the enquirer but exhibits little imagination. Patient and kind, this person loves animals and would make a good vetinarian. The card can represent the involvements concerned with the purchase of land or a house. Reversed, there can be irresponsibility and carelessness in work as well as idleness in the affairs concerning money.

SEXUAL ASPECTS: This is a person who keeps a mate by supplying sex that is always satisfying, who is attentive to a partner's needs.

REVERSED: A person who is preoccupied with their own orgasm. They can exhibit a narrowmindedness concerning the sex act that is a great disappoitment to the partner, manifesting a dullness and ordinariness in sex that is soulless.

THE 10 OF JADES:

DESCRIPTION: An elderly man is seated in a garden, talking to a woman. She could be his daughter. They are seated in front of a house and seem contented.

INTERPRETATION: The fullness of time. The completion of the circle of events. Property is purchased and finances become stable. The family is enjoyed and reunion is about to take place.

REVERSED: A chance fatality. The death of a relative or member of the immediate family. There can be theft or loss through hazardous business ventures. Difficulties over a will or other stippends.

SEXUAL EXPRESSION: Sexual riches. An abundance of pleasure from involvement with family, cousins and the like. Reversed, there is loss of virginity, loss of potency, or even loss of one's sexual partner.

THE 9 OF JADES:

DESCRIPTION: A beautifully dressed woman is commanding a bird to land where she wants.

INTERPRETATION: There is sucess and discernment in this life; however, something is missing. There is a solitariness about this card, even with its atmosphere of success and enjoyment of the good things of life.

REVERSED: There is the possibility of loss, either by theft or by legal involvements. A case may be won but the lawyers will get all of the money. There is bad faith here and caution is advised.

SEXUAL EXPRESSION: A lover who is not exciting but is true. Sexual desires that are only half satisfied. Sexual energy turned towards nurturing and growing things. Reversed, it changes little, perhaps an uneventful widowhood.

THE 8 OF JADES:

DESCRIPTION: A craftsman, good at his work, is putting the finishing touches to a jade. He is successful and many jades are completed and ready for sale.

INTERPRETATION: There is work about to be made available. An apprenticeship, a commission for an artist. Your skill is needed.

REVERSED: Biting off more than one can chew. There is vanity and exaggeration about abilities. There can be usury and cunning.

SEXUAL EXPRESSION: The beginnings of a fruitful sexual experience involving responsibility. Imagination in sexual foreplay. Reversed, there are vain and false promises voiced, also disillusion over ability to deliver promised sexual favors.

THE 7 OF JADES:

DESCRIPTION: A tree grows— one side is brown, the other side purple, its fruit are jades. A man is seen picking the fruit. In the tree's roots is hidden a skull.

INTERPRETATION: This is the money tree and is the card of all money-related matters, including loans, investments, and gambles. It is also a card that indicates a re-evaluation may be in order.

REVERSED: The skull shows its teeth. There is anxiety over a loan or concerning a business deal. Quarrel over money. Poor profit from a large investment. Care with stocks and bonds.

SEXUAL EXPRESSION: Sex for money is intended here. This is the card of the pimp and procurer of sexual favors for money. The barter of sex for the supply of material needs. Reversed, there is a withholding of sex, a cheating of the procurer, a pretending of excitement and passion. False expectations are revealed.

THE 6 OF JADES:

DESCRIPTION: A wealthy woman is pictured in the act of dispensing gifts to all. She seems contented and pleased with her largess.

INTERPRETATION: Now is the time to share that with which you are blessed. The questioner will undoubtedly receive a just reward. Time to give and receive presents.

REVERSED: A gift turns out to be a bribe. There is unfairness. A bank makes a mistake and refuses to acknowledge it. There can be envy of others and illusions about one's own value.

SEXUAL EXPRESSION: A much desired lover will come to one. There is sex indicated between people of different races. Reversed, there is jealousy and disruption between the partners.

THE 5 OF JADES:

DESCRIPTION: A wealthy man, who is crippled with disease and walks with a crutch and a staff, is stalked by a jaguar.

INTERPRETATION: This is the card of poor health. The constitution is delicate and needs protection. Care is required to guard against adversity. In spiritual quests, it is the "chapel perilous."

REVERSED: There is discord and waste. Disorder reigns. Conditions worsen before they get better but it is not total ruin.

SEXUAL EXPRESSION: An undesired pregnancy. A hysterectomy is requied by partner. Loss of sensitivity in the sexual act. Reversed, it can indicate that the desired mate has unrealized, or even active, homosexual tendencies. A marriage is threatened by a mistress.

THE 4 OF JADES:

DESCRIPTION: A wealthy man sits on a terrace in front of his house. He muses about a jade in his hand. There is another around his neck. Two more are hidden under his feet.

INTERPRETATION: A miserly person, mean or simply unable to realize that he is no longer poor. Hidden resources. Gift or legacy.

REVERSED: There are delays and holdups in business transactions. There could be opposition to a merger. Overextension of resources seems to be a problem. Uncertainty in the market place.

SEXUAL EXPRESSION: There is a definite holding on to present sex partners, for fear of a loss. Enjoyment of present benefits of a sexual nature. Reversed, there is danger of loss through seduction of the partner by neighbor or business partner. Care is required in guarding the virtue of another.

THE 3 OF JADES:

DESCRIPTION: A very wealthy man is donating jades to the temple. A craftsman is busy attaching them to the roof.

INTERPRETATION: The rewards of skill and ability are reaped. A patron is possibly in the offing. Material success and monetary gain are available. Artists receive a commission for important work.

REVERSED: Delays in signing a much desired contract. Work will suffer because of a preoccupation with money. Ideas may be purile and petty.

SEXUAL EXPRESSION: A single person gains a reputation as a fabulous sex partner and is much in demand. Reversed, sexual creativity and ability are undermined by mediocrity of technique and lack of interest.

THE 2 OF JADES:

DESCRIPTION: A very handsome and beautifully dressed black man balances two jades. He seems to be juggling them. He kneels on a yellow mat. Behind him is a turbulent stream.

INTERPRETATION: The maintaining of balance and harmony in the midst of changing times. The handling of several deals at one time. Gaiety, recreation, or a vacation is possible.

REVERSED: Too many irons in the fire. Plans are hard to manipulate. Things are forced and strained. There is no leeway.

SEXUAL EXPRESSION: Gaiety and carefree sexual relations. Parties where sexual games are played. Sexual "fun and frolic." A wonderful affair that one knows cannot last, but one doesn't care. Reversed, it reads as above but the gaiety is forced. The party is really a drag. Lots of sex, but who cares?

THE 1 OF JADES:

DESCRIPTION: A large jade entwined by a snake. It rests among flowers, the bounty of nature. There is a sun sign, an olin sign, which means movement, and a sprouted maize seed.

INTERPRETATION: This is the card of prosperity. Prosperous times are ahead. Things are improving rapidly. There is contentment with the way life evolves and changes. Goodness and light.

REVERSED: Greed and the evil side of wealth are represented here. Comfort and material conditions lead to corruption. The seed falls on barren ground.

SEXUAL EXPRESSION: There is complete happiness and contentment with the sexual partner. Sex is beautiful and joy abounds. Reversed, this card turns sex into a grasping and unpleasant pastime. There is corruption for money.

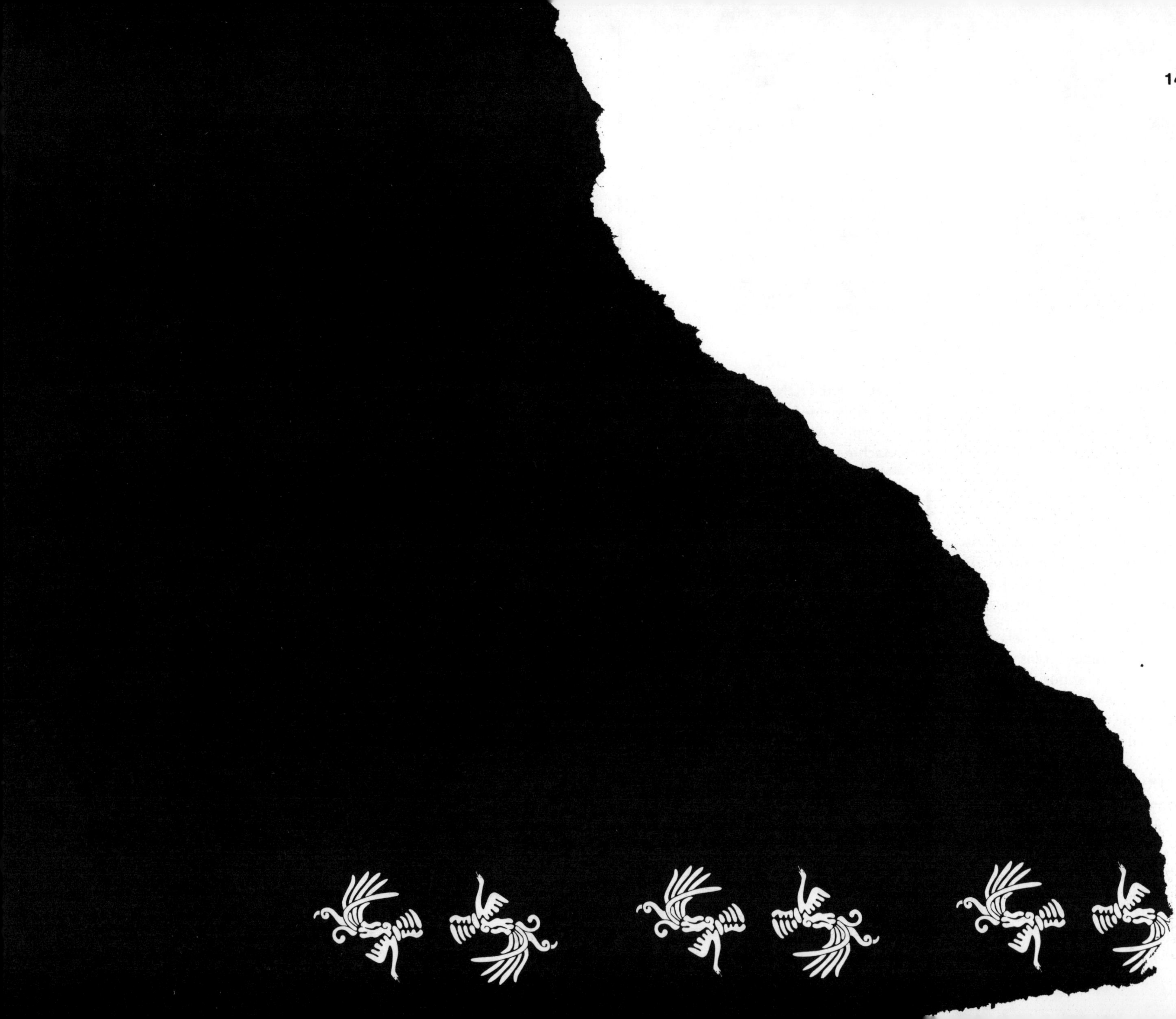

THE·JOURNEY·OF·THE·FOOL

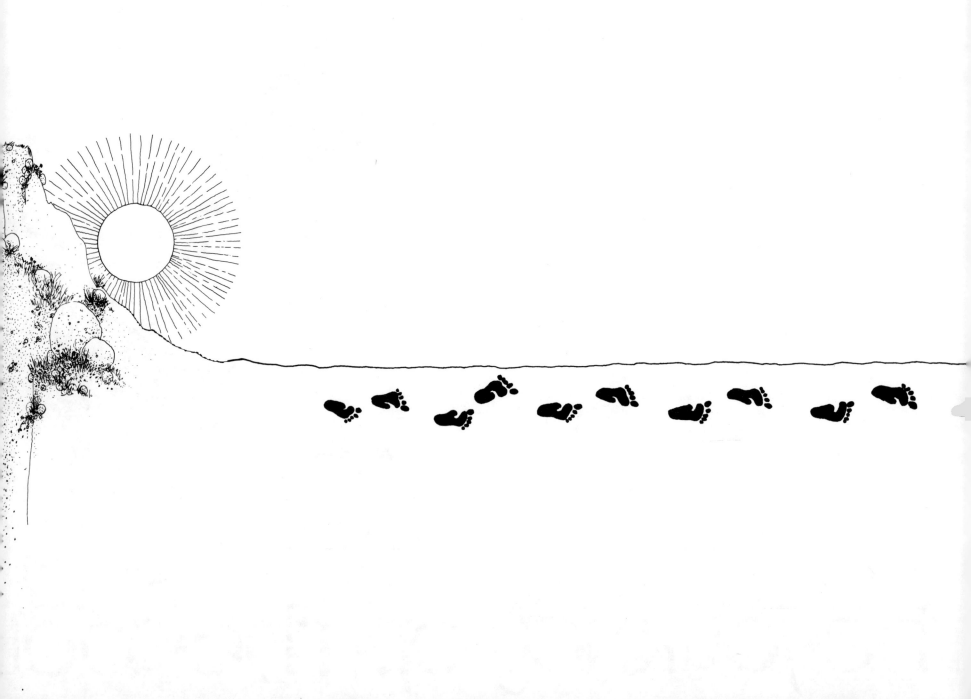

TEXT AND ILLUSTRATIONS
BY PETER BALIN

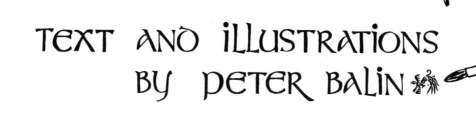

YOU ⬚ STAND ⬚ THERE TREMBLING ⬚ ON ⬚ THE ABYSS

ARE ⬚ YOU ⬚ SEARCHING THE ⬚ DAYS ⬚ OF ⬚ YOUR YOUTH?

ARE ⬚ YOU ⬚ LOOKING FOR ⬚ THE ⬚ TIME ⬚ OF YOUR ⬚ LIFE?

THE N ⬚ LIVE ⬚ BEYOND ⬚ THE ⬚ MINUTE ⬚ & ⬚ THE ⬚ HOUR ⬚ IN ⬚ TIME ⬚ WHERE ⬚ NO ⬚ CLOCK ⬚ WORKS & ⬚ NO ⬚ DAY ⬚ DAWNS

IN ⬚ THAT ⬚ PLACE ⬚ WHERE ⬚ FREEDOMS ⬚ YEARS PASS ⬚ THE ⬚ END

LESS ⬡⬡ SUCCESSIONS OF ⬡ NOT ⬡ SUNS ⬡⬡ RISINGS OF ⬡ NOT ⬡ EARTHS ⬡ TURNINGS

BUT OF ⬡ MINDS ⬡ OPENING OF ⬡ HUMANS ⬡ BEING

IN ⬡ LOVE ⬡⬡ KNOWING ⬡ WHERE ORANGES ⬡ & ⬡ THE SUN ⬡⬡

HAVE ⬡⬡ MIRACLES IN ⬡⬡ COMMON ⬡⬡

WHAT ⬡ ⬡⬡ YOU ⬡⬡ ⬡ SEEK IS WRITTEN ⬡ & ⬡ NOTHING ⬡⬡ HIDDEN ⬡⬡ YOU ⬡⬡ ARE ⬡ THE ⬡ BOOK

⬡⬡ SEARCH ⬡⬡ THE ⬡⬡ SELF ⬡ THEN ⬡ SHALL ⬡ SECRETS ⬡ STAND ⬡ REVEALED

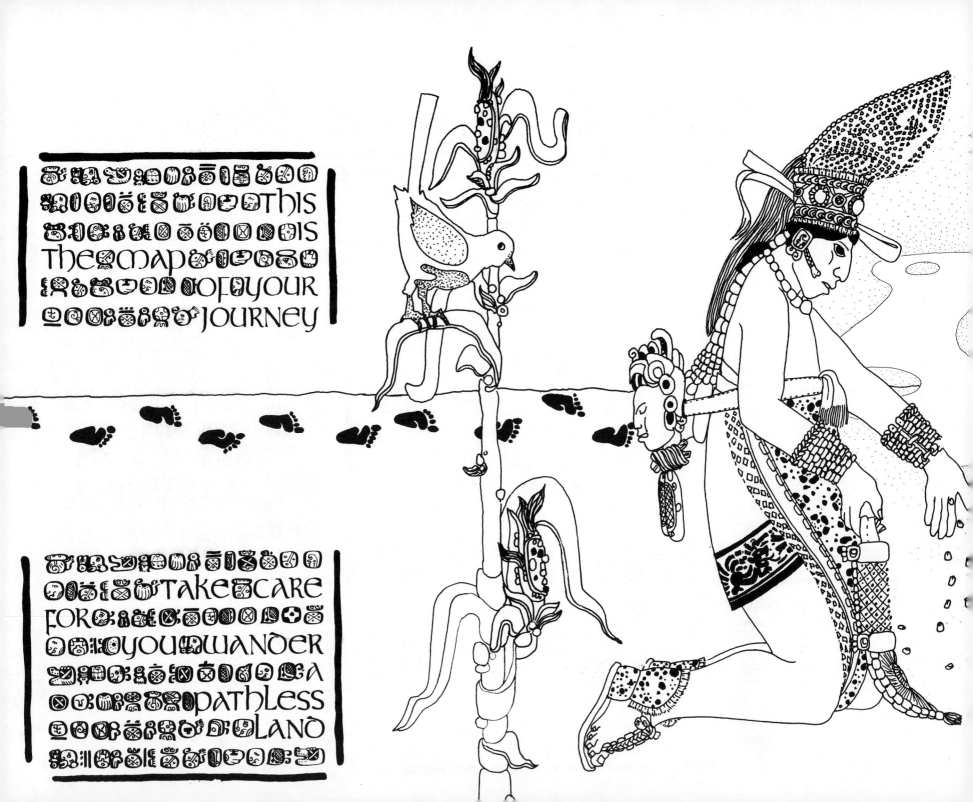

THIS IS THE MAP OF YOUR JOURNEY

TAKE CARE FOR YOU WANDER A PATHLESS LAND

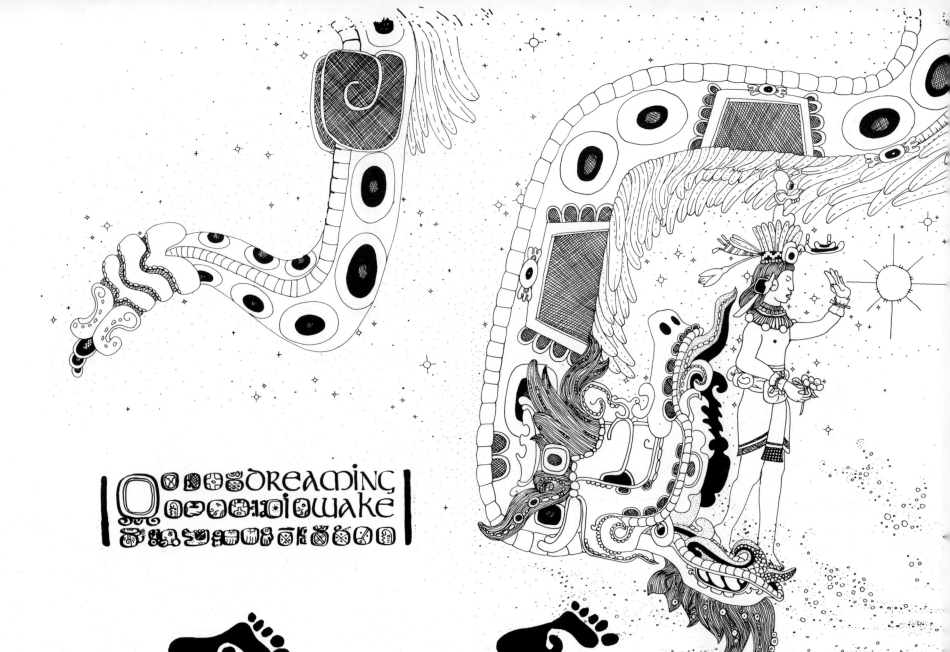

DREAMING I WAKE

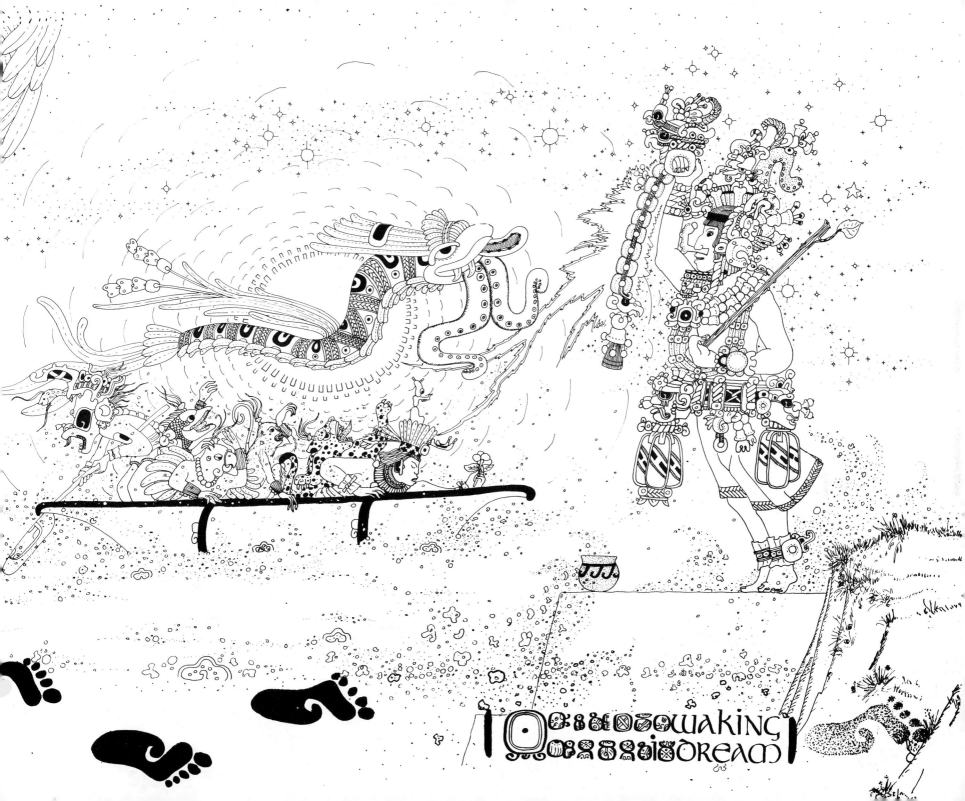

PAST IS THE FUTURE NOW

LOVE
IS
ACTION
ALL
ELSE
IS
REACTION

TRADITION
LEARNED WITH LOVE I

ENTER THE HOUSE OF MIND SEE MYSTERIES WITHIN

TAKE CARE

YOU WANDERER

THE JOY YOU SEEK IS LOCKED WITHIN YOUR LIMITATIONS YOUR PLEASURES ARE THE ONLY SEAL

YOUR DREAM IS YOUR END

THE GODS GATHERED IN DARKNESS & MADE THE WORLD

Let there be light!
So the dawn shall rise over heavens
And the Earth.

There can be no glory, no splendour,
Until the human being exists
As the fully developed person.

Popol Vuh.

LOVE
AND
LIGHT

A SHORT BIOGRAPHY OF THE
PAINTER OF THE XULTUN TAROT DECK

Peter Balin was born in New Zealand and has lived in many countries, among them India, Italy, England, and France. He lived in Brazil for three years and at various other times in Guatemala, Mexico, and Belize.

He has earned his living in different occupations, primarily as a carpenter and a teacher (sometimes of spoken English and at other times of woodwork and arts and crafts). This is probably all explained by the fact that he is a Gemini, with the Sun, the Moon, and Mercury all in Gemini. He was born on the fifth of June 1932. Peter now makes his home in Los Angeles, where he has lived for the past six years.

The Cards had their beginning at 10:30 p.m. on the night of December 21st, 1975. Three friends—Margaret Johnson, Brett Forray, and David Biedekapp—visited Peter and brought a tarot deck with them. Peter was not impressed with the deck. It was the first deck he had ever seen and he considered it medieval, superstitious nonsense. When Margaret suggested he should paint a tarot deck, he did not waste words about what a silly idea he thought that to be. In the middle of his tirade he suddenly saw a tarot deck in Maya Indian dress with all of the cards of the higher Arcana joined together to form one picture. The next day he began to paint the deck. It took three months and he worked night and day at it. Eleven months after the night of the 21st of December, the cards were on the market.

The deck has many unique features. It is the first deck with its roots in the Americas. All other decks have a European origin. It is the only deck in existence that fits together to make one picture, clearly demonstrating the interdependence and the inseparability of all life forms.

Peter Balin is pleased to be able to add his small contribution toward making people aware of the great religious tradition of the native Americans. He feels that the Western world has a lot to learn from the peoples whose civilization they so barbariously decimated.

For those persons that are interested in astrology, two charts are presented below without comment. The first is the birth chart of Peter Balin, the other is a chart drawn up for the time the cards were first conceived.

ASTROLOGICAL BIRTH CHART FOR JUNE 5, 1932, 2:30 A.M.

174 E. 07.   39 S. 33.

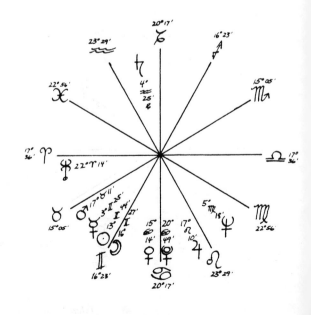

ASTROLOGICAL CHART FOR DEC. 21, 1975, 10:30 P.M.

118 W. 15.   34 N. 3.5

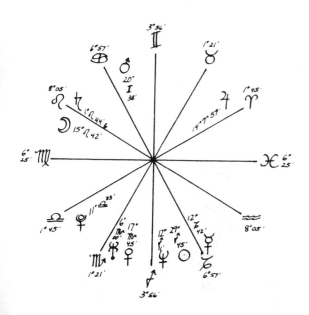

Glen Dixon

THE MAYAS:

BURNING WATER.

Laurette Sejourne.
Shambala Publications Inc.
Berkeley.

MAYA HISTORY AND RELIGION.

J. Eric S. Thompson.
University of Oklahoma Press.

MEXICO MYSTIQUE.

Frank Waters.
The Swallow Press Inc. Chicago.

THE POPOL VUH OF THE QUICHE MAYA.

Munro S. Edmonson.
Tulane University Press. New Orleans.

THE BOOK OF CHILAM BALAM.

Ralph L. Roys.
University of Oklahoma Press.

THE BRAIN:

USE BOTH SIDES OF YOUR BRAIN.

Tony Buzan.
E.P. Dutton & Co. Inc.

THE ORIGIN OF CONSCIOUSNESS IN THE BREAKDOWN OF THE BICAMERAL MIND.

Julian Jaynes.
Houghton Mifflin Company.
Boston.

NOVELS:

THE MAGUS.

John Fowles.
Dell Publishing Co. Inc. N.Y.

NOVA

Samual R. Delany.
Bantam Science Fiction.

THE TAROT:

THE ROYAL ROAD.

Stephan A. Hoeller.
Quest Books Wheaton, Ill.

THE ENCYCLOPEDIA OF TAROT.

Stuart R. Kaplan.
U.S. Games Systems. N.Y.

TAROT CLASSIC.

Stuart R. Kaplan.
U.S. Games Systems. N.Y.

THE TAROT.

Alfred Douglas.
Penguin Books Ltd. Maryland.

THE TAROT.

Manly P. Hall.
The Philosophical Research Society, Los Angeles.

THE TAROT.

Paul Foster Case.
Macoy Publishing Company.
Richmond, Virginia.